SCOTTISH STEAM ROUTES

ROGER SIVITER

BLOOMSBURY BOOKS
LONDON

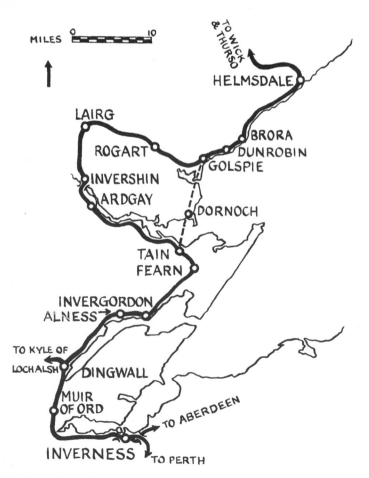

On Sunday 31 August 1986, Class 5MT 4-6-0 No 44767 *George Stephenson* crosses the Kyle of Sutherland at Invershin with a special train from Inverness to Helmsdale on the Wick/Thurso route, the first time that steam has run on this line for well over twenty years. This train, which was organised jointly by ScotRail and the Scottish Railway Preservation Society, was run mainly to test out the radio signalling equipment on a steam locomotive in preparation for the Fort William-Mallaig line, which goes over to this system in 1987.

This steam run, which could be the only one on this route, came about after this book was virtually finished and at the printers. That is the reason that there is no section in the book on this line, but fortunately the publisher was able to include at least one picture.

There is a plan to build a combined road and rail bridge across the Dornoch Firth, laying a new line from Tain through Dornoch to Golspie. This would bypass Invershin. However, the plan also considers the possibility of keeping the Invershin route open to Lairg.

Introduction

For railway enthusiasts the rail routes in Scotland provide a fascinating contrast from the busy inter city lines between Glasgow and Edinburgh through to the splendour and beauty of the West Highland and Kyle of Lochalsh lines. Indeed the steam enthusiast is very fortunate in Scotland because there has been and still is steam motive power on special trains on a great many lines.

Scottish railways can boast some of the finest scenery in the world as well as some of the most spectacular engineering feats, notably the Forth and Tay railway bridges. Surely the Forth Bridge must rank as one of the most beautiful bridges ever built and a triumph of man's engineering genius.

There are still many fine stations and railway buildings in Scotland and at most stations large or small there is a pride in the job as indeed there is throughout the whole of the region at all levels of work. This is well in evidence from the spick and span appearance of most of the motive power and rolling stock, some with the new ScotRail liveries.

Also, for the time being there is still a certain amount of semaphore signalling and many fine old signal boxes, some dating from pre-grouping days.

Scotland is also the home for many famous preserved steam locomotives notably John Cameron's LNER A4 Pacific No 60009 *Union of South Africa,* the Scottish Railway Preservation Society's North British 0-6-0 *Maude,* LNER 4-4-0 *Morayshire* and Caledonian 0-4-4 tank No 419 and Class 5MT 4-6-0 No 5025 of the Strathspey Railway at Aviemore, which together with many visiting locomotives are the main features of this book. Also featured are some of the many popular types of diesel locomotives that have worked and are still working on the Scottish Region – including the sadly missed Deltic and Class 40s as well as Class 26, 27, 37, 47, and many others. On some sections I have also included a few pictures from 'steam days' on BR. Even in the last few years of BR steam Scotland had a very rich variety of locomotives from pre-grouping goods locomotives to LNER A2 and A4 Pacifics on the Aberdeen-Glasgow three hour expresses.

In conclusion I should like to thank the many people, without whose help a project like this would be impossible, the many photographers who have put their collections at my disposal, Joan Wappett for the typing, my wife Christina for the maps and help with the layout, my publishers for complete freedom in the layout and choice of material, and finally and most important of all to the railwaymen (professional and amateur) who make it all possible.

Note: Unless specified all photographs were taken by the author.

This edition published 1988 by
Bloomsbury Books an imprint of
Godfrey Cave Associates Limited
42 Bloomsbury Street, London WC1B 3QJ
under licence from Baton Transport/
Cleveland Press

ISBN 1 870630 06 8

Printed in Yugoslavia

Some other Bloomsbury Books titles
Metroland Trilogy
by Denis Edwards & Ron Pigram
1. Metro Memories
2. Romance of Metroland
3. The Golden Years of Metropolitan Railway

Settle to Carlisle by Roger Siviter
Welsh Marches by Roger Siviter

Down the Line Series titles include:
Dover, Southend, Bristol and Brighton.

SECTION ONE

CARLISLE — KILMARNOCK — AYR — WATERSIDE — GLASGOW

Our journey starts in Carlisle Citadel station under the wires. This is the former Caledonian line over Beattock summit to Carstairs, and was shared by the Glasgow and South-Western as far as Gretna. The Waverley route (North British) used to start from the west side of Citadel station and cross over, north of the station, heading north-east. We cross the River Eden, and run through Kingmoor, the diesel depot. At Gretna junction the electrified line continues north while we turn west on the ex-G & SW line; to the east an industrial spur is all that remains of the North British connection to Longtown, a junction on the Waverley route.

We follow the north shore of the Solway Firth to Annan station, passing the Eastriggs industrial spur on the left. At Annan, there used to be a Caledonian line which crossed from Bowness in Cumbria by the Solway viaduct to join the Carstairs line at Kirtlebridge. This crossed our line, with connecting spurs. To the south-west of Annan we can see Criffel mountain, 1868 ft, rising from the shore behind Sweetheart Abbey.

At Dunfries, which is famous as Robert Burns' home town, a spur runs west from the station to the depots at Maxwellton, part of the former G & SW line to Kirkudbright. A branch used to run off this, the Portpatrick and Wigtownshire, from Castle Douglas to Stranraer and Portpatrick. The station does credit to the town in the delightful brackets of the canopies and in the display of flowers.

We leave the rich farmlands with their herds of Banded Galloways and follow the River Nith northwest into the Lowther Hills, up gradients of 1 in 150. We pass the former stations of Thornhill and Carronbridge. At Enoch, a Roman road takes the pass northeast to Elvanfoot, while on the left, a pink 17th century castle called Drumlanrig gives its name to the mile long tunnel ahead.

Still climbing, we pass through the closed station of Sanquhar and cross Crawick water by a round-arched viaduct. After Kirkconnel station, we follow the Nith as it turns westwards. Just before New Cumnock, now closed, the gradient eases off on the moorland watershed, and there used to be troughs here. At Bank junction there is now a short southward spur to Knockshinnock. Our line snakes north over Polquhap summit where the notorious Blackfaulds cutting often fills with snow, then through the site of Old Cumnock station. A busy G & SW line used to intersect here, which came from Belstone junction in the west to connect with a Caledonian line from Carstairs in the east.

The line descends as much as 1 in 145 to Auchinleck where a station is proposed. A spur runs to Barony colliery to the west. At Brackenhill junction there used to be a branch to Catrine. The line crosses the River Ayr on the imposing Ballochmyle viaduct, then reaches Mauchline junction. This serves a goods line that runs down to Newton on Ayr on the coast. Halfway down is Annbank junction where the Killoch colliery spur joins in.

A short rise brings us to Mossgiel tunnel. The wind sweeps this stretch of moorland so that the telegraph poles have to be buttressed. A mile or so beyond used to be Garrochburn goods depot, after which we drop 1 in 100 past a spur to a distillery on the right, down to Hurlford. This used to be an important shed for Kilmarnock. Just before the viaduct, a G & SW line used to pass underneath from Troon on the coast to connect with a Caledonian line running from the Monklands colliery complex. Part of this junction at Kay Park survives as a spur to Riccarton BP depot.

Kilmarnock used to have a locomotive works, supplementing St Rollox. It was the first signal centre in the area to use telephone control instead of block tokens in 1925. In the station, the canopy brackets show the company initials in the cast-iron roundels. Just after the station, a single track branches left through the site of St Marnocks station and runs for about eight miles west down to Barassie junction on the coastal line. This partly follows the very first Scottish line, a 4 ft gauge waggon way built by the Duke of Portland in 1812 to carry coal from St Marnocks to Troon. Five years later, Stephenson was using his second steam engine from Killingworth in Northumbria to haul the Duke's coal trains.

The coastal line runs from Largs through Ardrossan and Ayr to the ferry at Stranraer for Larne in Ireland. The boat train from Glasgow St Enoch used to be called "The Paddy". We join this line and run south from Barassie junction through Troon. The passenger station lies in a loop on the seaward side, and a spur runs to the harbour. The through route runs past the college overlooking the sidings.

Approaching Prestwick we see a golf course in the dunes, and an airport to the east. Just before the station, a line used to connect with Annbank junction on the line to Mauchline from Newton on Ayr, our next station. We

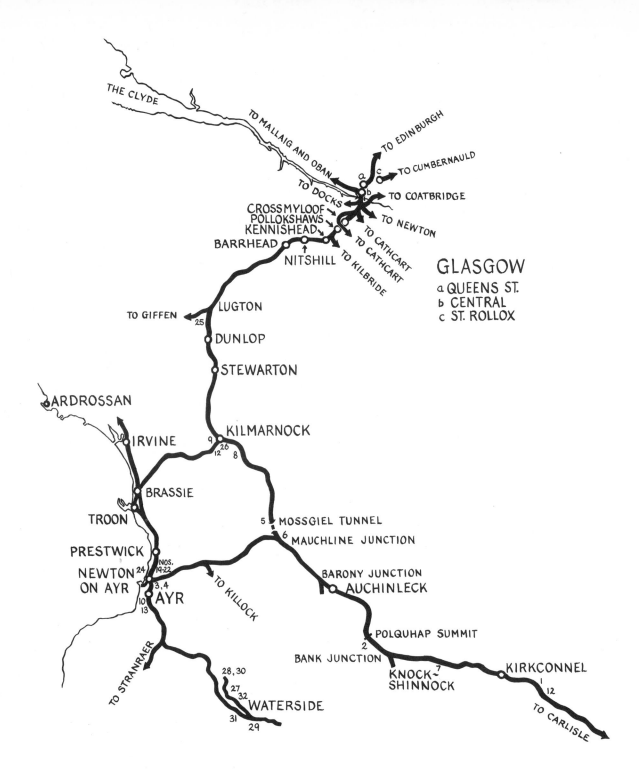

pass through Falklands junction and Harbour junction, both giving onto the docks at the mouth of the River Ayr and enclosing Newton station. Just after, the A79 crosses our line by the signal box for the goods line to Mauchline. The triangle of this junction encloses the Newtonhead coal depot where the locomotive shed used to be.

The line crosses the River Ayr by a stone arched viaduct and passes through Ayr station next to the hospital. South of here the line was originally planned only to reach Girvan to develop it as a potato growing district, Stranraer then being served by the south coast route. Two routes from Ayr met at Girvan; the closed coastal line ran through Alloway, Burns' birthplace, and the inland one survives today. From Dalrymple junction, four miles south of Ayr station, the Dalmellington branch turns east and crosses the spectacular Dalrymple viaduct to stop at Waterside colliery on the banks of the

River Doon. This line has gradients of 1 in 70.

Returning to Kilmarnock, the former G & SW line running straight ahead to Dalry junction is now closed, but we take the single track northwards past the John Walker's distillery to Kilmaurs. This line was jointly owned by the Caledonian and the G & SW, after they saw the folly of duplicating lines. We climb the 1 in 87 to Stewarton station and up the 1 in 75 to the summit on Gameshill just before Dunlop station. Descending slightly we run through the former station at Lugton with its passing loop and the junction for the line to the Admiralty establishment at Giffen, six miles west. This line, and a short spur to the east, are remains of a Caledonian line that ran from Ardrossan and from Kilbirnie via Giffen junction to Neilston and Cathcart in the north east – the twin of the duplicated lines mentioned earlier.

Now on ex-G & SW rails, we top the summit at Shilford and run down the 1 in 67 to Barrhead station where our line becomes double track again. This rapid descent takes us from moorland into the suburban network of Glasgow. After Nitshill and Kennishead stations, the line from East Kilbride joins us from the east at Busby junction. We pass through Pollockshaws West station and run underneath the circular route from Cathcart. After Crossmyloof, at the former station at Strathbungo a goods line branches east, while the Cathcart line circles in from the west. Another goods line turns off west linking with Paisley and the docks to the west, and with Mossend to the east. We pass over this line, then another linking spur comes in from the east. We pass under a goods loop running from the Paisley line (via Shields junction) to Coatbridge (via High St junction). The Paisley passenger line joins us at Bridge St junction, then we cross over the River Clyde and run into Glasgow Central station. The line formerly terminated at Bridge Street. The Clyde Bridge was built by William Arrol in 1879, and was 700 feet long and carried four tracks. The new eight-track bridge was opened in 1905.

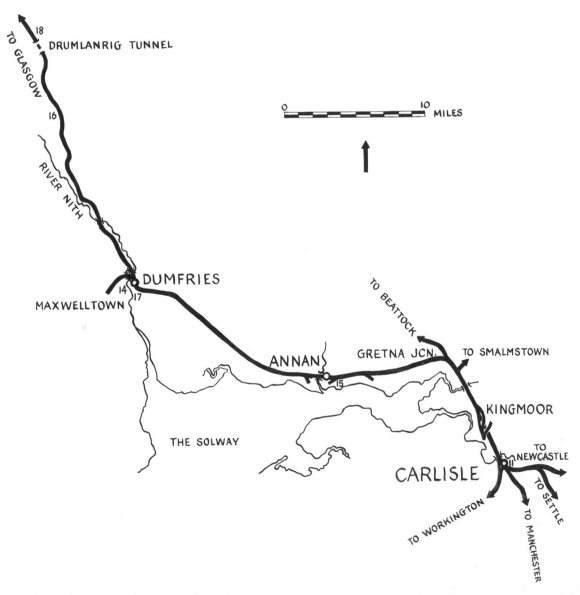

1. *Above* On 20 April 1985 Jubilee Class 4-6-0 No 5690 *Leander* ran a special train from Kilmarnock to Hellifield, this was organised by the Steam Locomotive Operators' Association (SLOA). The steam special is seen heading south on the G&SW route between Kirkonnel and Sanquhar. K. J. C. JACKSON

2. *Below* Another view of the above train, this time as it approaches New Cumnock. *The Thames–Clyde Express* headboard is very apt for this train. In LMS days this was the principal express between London St Pancras and Glasgow, running over the Settle–Carlisle route and then the old Glasgow and South Western route to Glasgow. BRIAN DOBBS

3 and 4. Contrast at Falkland Junction to the north of Ayr. In the top picture we see preserved Class 40 No D200 with an Ayr to Carlisle special on 22 October 1983. K. J. C. JACKSON

In the bottom picture John Cameron's famous A4 pacific No 60009 *Union of South Africa* hurries along with *The Sou-Wester Express* bound for Carlisle. 10 March 1984. JOHN LAVERICK

All Ayr to Carlisle passenger trains now run via Kilmarnock. For many years they joined the G&SWR main line to Carlisle at Mauchline junction some ten miles to the south of Kilmarnock. This line from Ayr to Mauchline branches off the Ayr–Kilmarnock line a mile north of Ayr station and is now used for goods traffic only.

5. *Top left* No 5690 approaches Mossgiel tunnel, some two miles to the north of Mauchline with the Kilmarnock–Hellifield special of 20 April 1985. Soon after leaving Kilmarnock southbound trains face gradients of around 1 in 100 for five miles up to Mossgiel tunnel. *Leander* appears to be in no trouble at all as it nears the summit of the climb. LES NIXON

6. *Bottom left* This picturesque scene shows North British 0-6-0 *Maude* heading south near Mauchline on 17 May 1980 with a special from Kilmarnock to Manchester for the Liverpool and Manchester 150th Anniversary Celebrations at Rainhill. LES NIXON

7. *Above* No 46229 *Duchess of Hamilton* and the National Railway Museum's LNWR BFK No 5155 make their way south from the Ayr Railfair (of 29/30 October) on Monday 31 October 1983. They were photographed between New Cumnock and Kirkconnel. TOM NOBLE

8. *Below Leander* and the Kilmarnock–Hellifield special of 20 April 1985 are seen as they leave Hurlford at the start of the stiff climb up to Mossgiel tunnel. This location is a mile to the south of Kilmarnock. JOHN LAVERICK

9. *Above* No 673 0-6-0 *Maude* pictured at Kilmarnock on the morning of 17 May 1980 prior to working a special to Manchester. LES NIXON

10. *Top right* Ayr motive power depot on the evening of 13 September 1985. LES NIXON

11. *Bottom right* Carlisle station on a very wet evening – 28 December 1983. Class 26 No 26036 waits to leave with the 1720 to Glasgow via Annan and Kilmarnock on the G&SW route.

Although not in Scotland Carlisle is regarded as the gateway to that famous country.

12. *Above* Class 24 No 24105 enters Kilmarnock on 21 May 1974 with an Ayr–Carlisle parcels train.

These type 2 locomotives introduced in 1958 have long since been scrapped but happily three of the class have been preserved. The splendid semaphore signals at Kilmarnock have also been scrapped and replaced by colour light signalling. TOM HEAVYSIDE

13. *Below* Pulling out of Ayr on 25 August 1981 in charge of the daily parcels train to Stranraer is Class 27 No 27032. Note the fine station building behind the locomotive. LES NIXON

14. *Above* The fine old station at Dumfries provides an attractive frame for *Union of South Africa* as it waits for the Class 37 to hook on to the train for the journey to Carlisle. 14 September 1985. The train is a special from Edinburgh to Leeds.

Diesel motive power is nearly always provided for steam specials for the final section to Carlisle as trains have to run the final ten miles from Gretna junction to Carlisle under the wires. K. J. C. JACKSON

15. *Below* Class 47/4 No 47540 pauses at Annan on 1 November 1984 with the 1100 Stranraer–Euston. Since the closure of the direct line from Stranraer to Dumfries trains now have to travel via Ayr and Kilmarnock. TOM HEAVYSIDE

16. *Above* On a dull 10 March 1984 No 60009 provides a stirring sight as it heads south for Carlisle with *The Sou-Wester Express*. The location is near Thornhill and the 'wrong line' working is probably due to engineering works. JOHN COOPER-SMITH

17 and 18. *Right* Two views of *Maude* on 17 May 1980 on its historic journey from Kilmarnock to Manchester.

In the top picture the train is shown hurrying away from Dumfries and in the bottom view the train is shown in a picturesque setting on the approach to Drumlanrig tunnel in the Nith Valley. LES NIXON

These next four scenes were taken at Newton on Ayr on 18 August 1983. This location is a mile to the north of Ayr station and is the junction for the Ayr Harbour branch.

19. *Top left* Class 27 No 27101 heads south through the station at Newton on Ayr en route to the motive power depot.

20. *Bottom left* A string of empty coal wagons is hauled up from the Harbour branch by class 20s Nos 20213 and 20011, no doubt heading for one of the collieries situated to the south and east of Ayr.

21. *Right* Class 37 No 37051 hurries the 1315 Stranraer Harbour–Glasgow train through Newton on Ayr.

22. *Below* A rake of full coal wagons hauled by Class 27 No 27055 comes off the goods only line from Mauchline junction, crosses the main Ayr-Glasgow and Kilmarnock line and heads down the Ayr Harbour branch for a waiting collier.

23. *Above* LNER Pacific No 4472 *Flying Scotsman* is pictured south of Kirkconnel on 22 October 1983 as it heads northwards with a SLOA special from Annan–Ayr. The excursion originated at Euston.
TOM NOBLE

24. *Left Union of South Africa* accelerates through Newton on Ayr with the Sou-Wester Express for Carlisle. 10 March 1984. JOHN COOPER-SMITH

25. *Top right* Lugton junction, some fifteen miles south of Glasgow is the setting for the 1730 Glasgow–Carlisle train hauled by Class 47/4 No 47462. The date is 18 August 1983.
  Lugton is the junction for the goods only line to Giffen. The line from Glasgow to Kilmarnock was originally the Glasgow, Barrhead & Kilmarnock Joint later Caledonian and Glasgow & South Western.

26. *Bottom right* Class 5MT 4-6-0 No 44767 *George Stephenson* at Kilmarnock station on 22 March 1986 before departure for Glasgow Eastfield depot, from where it will travel to Fort William for work on the West Highland Line (section seven). BRIAN DOBBS

South west Scotland is noted for its scenery and rich farming land and Ayrshire is also noted for its collieries where until the mid 1970s steam traction was still at work. The most famous of these being the Waterside system some ten miles to the south east of Ayr on the Dalmellington branch.

The line to Waterside, which leaves the Stranraer line at Dalrymple junction is still open for goods traffic.

The next three pages show industrial steam at work on this very fine system.

27. *Top* No 24 an outside cylindered 0-6-0 tank built by Andrew Barclay in 1953 (works number 2335) shunts at Minnivey colliery (Waterside) on 30 August 1973. This locomotive is fitted with a Giesl ejector.

28. *Bottom* Shunting in the yard at Dunaskin on 5 August 1975 are No 17 0-6-0 tank built in 1913 by Barclays (works number 1338) and 0-4-0 saddle tank No 10 built by Barclays in 1947 (works number 2244).

This system ran from Pennyvenie and Minnivey collieries (in the southeast) for three and a half miles northwestwards to Dunaskin coal preparation plant.

29. *Top right* No 19 (Barclay 0-4-0 tank built in 1918 works number 1614) heads for the washerie at Dunaskin on 30 August 1973.

30. *Bottom right* No 10 throws out a good exhaust as it shunts at Dunaskin on 5 August 1975. Note the old style coal wagons.

31. *Above* The Waterside line ran through some very pleasant scenery as can be seen in this picture of No 19 as it heads for Dunaskin on 30 August 1973. The location is a mile to the north west of Minnivey colliery.

32. *Below* Waterside silhouette as No 19 shunts on the spoil tip. 30 August 1973.

SECTION TWO

GLASGOW — FALKIRK — EDINBURGH
EDINBURGH CIRCLE

The first routes were cobbled together from colliery lines in the Monklands fields around Coatbridge. A fast trunk route was built by the North British, opened 21 February 1842, which ran round the north side. This followed the Forth-Clyde canal from Glasgow to Grangemouth, opened in 1740, and the Union Canal from Falkirk to Edinburgh. This had very gentle gradients apart from its Queen St terminus in Glasgow. The canal proprietors refused permission to bridge their canal, so the Cowlairs incline (1 in 41) and tunnel had to be dug underneath it. The first trains had to be assisted with rope pulleys. The canal is now filled in to carry the M8, while the western end terminates near Cowlairs at Port Dundas by the power station.

At Cowlairs junction, a line goes past Sighthill to St Rollox to the east, and to the west a line runs to the West Highlands. We pass under the bridge of the disused Caledonian "north circular" route and reach Bishopbriggs station. We run straight northeast between the A80 to the south and the F & C canal and the Roman Antonine Wall, built AD142, which lie to the north. At the goods yard by Lochgrog, a colliery line used to join from the south.

After Lenzie station by a church steeple, we reach the closed station at Campsie. This was a junction for the NB line from Coatbridge to Kirkintilloch to the north. Originally there was a colliery line of 4' 6" or "Scotch" gauge carrying coal and iron ore from Monklands to the canal. The wagons used to be shipped entire onto canal barges, the forerunners of freightliners. The former junction at Waterside was the most eastern point of the Campsie complex, by the bridge over Luggie Water.

At Croy station we enter a mile-long cutting, coming out at the closed station of Dullatur. We cross the Antonine Wall which shadows the canal most of the way. With an airfield and Cumbernauld on our right we approach the former station at Castle Cary and cross in quick succession the Wall, the A80 dual carriageway and the ex-Caledonian line from Coatbridge to Stirling.

Greenhill Upper junction divides our line for the two Falkirk stations. The Coatbridge-Stirling line joins into the northern loop at Greenhill Lower junction. We pass through Carmuirs West junction where the left fork leads to Stirling, while the right fork leads to Falkirk Grahamston station, ex-North British. A goods line also used to run south through the former Falkirk Camelon station, ex-Caledonian, and underneath to Falkirk High. The Denny spur also used to run west connecting with a joint line to Kilsyth.

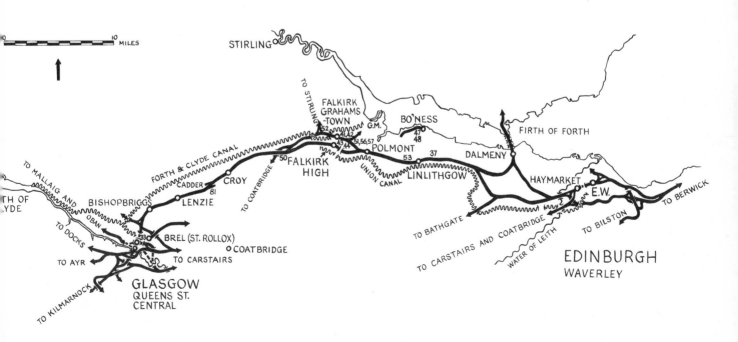

Where we cross the canal just before Grahamston station, a line used to run from Swingbridge junction – Lock 16 being the hub of the industrial network – to the iron foundries at Carron, using the hot blast smelters invented by James Beaumont Neilson in 1828. Just after Grahamston station, an ex-Caledonian spur runs north to Springfield yard and the oil refineries at Grangemouth docks.

From Greenhill Upper junction, the ex-North British line takes the southern route through Falkirk High station. Then at Greenbank we run along the north side of the head of the Union Canal, both passing through tunnels to emerge together at the former Redding Goods station. At Polmont junction the northern loop rejoins us. At Polmont station, there used to be a shed and a complex junction for a crossing line formerly from Slamannan to the south to Borrowstouness to the north. The port at "Bo'ness" fell into decline as canal and rail reached the deep water harbour at Grangemouth. The attractive private steam line now runs between Bo'ness and Kinniel by the end of the Wall.

We cross the River Avon, with its weirs and old waukmill, on Linlithgow viaduct and run through the station by the loch and palace. After the closed station of Philpstoun we lose sight of the canal and the M9 as we enter three miles of cuttings, pierced only where Winchburgh sends a goods cut-off loop to the Forth Bridge. We turn southeast through Winchburgh tunnel under the town and emerge near Niddrie castle on the left. This overlooks the vale of the River Almond which we cross on Telford's viaduct of 36 stone arches.

From Newbridge junction, a spur comes in from Bathgate car terminal in the west, formerly a line from Coatbridge. Wimpey have a depot on the south side of the station. We cross the M9 and reach the closed station of Ratho where a line used to run north to the Forth Bridge past Edinburgh airport. We pass another Sighthill, then the Inverkeithing line joins us from the north. After the golf course on the left was the junction for the former Corstorphine branch.

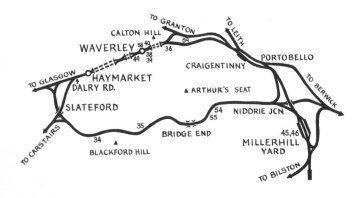

The Edinburgh Circle
Opposite the rugby ground a goods line comes in from the south, then we pass under the disued Caledonian bridge for Leith and Granton docks, one-time ferry station for Burntisland and Stirling. In 1845 there were moves to build an atmospheric railway to Leith. The ex-Caledonian line from Carstairs comes in from the south then we run past the former Haymarket shed, now a coal

depot, then through Haymarket station and into Haymarket tunnel some two-thirds of a mile long. We emerge below St Cuthbert's church and the Caledonian hotel to the north and Edinburgh castle to the south.

The line through Princess St Gardens was originally two tracks; two more tracks and their separate tunnels were allowed by Act of Parliament 5 July 1891 to relieve the congestion, which remained heavy until the electrification of the tramways in 1922 and the introduction of motor buses.

Ahead two tunnels run under the Mound, in fact a great spoil tip, now carrying the National Gallery (in Ionic style) and the Royal Institution (in Doric). We emerge into Edinburgh Waverley station overlooked by the Scott Monument and the North British hotel on north side, and the Castle and St Giles Cathedral on the south, and boxed-in by North Bridge and Waverley Bridge. The concourse is delightful, and lit by a glazed dome "lantern" in the ceiling surrounded by moulded festoons. At the east end, built on the site of Waverley market and the Botanical gardens, the new staff quarters have been built on a disused bay; the tinted glass casing makes it almost invisible.

On leaving Waverley on the passenger line we run below the Nelson column and "Scotland's Shame", the half-finished monument to the fallen in the Peninsular wars, then we run half-a-mile under the hill through Calton tunnel. A former goods line to Granton now only goes to Albert St depot, from Abbeyhill junction and from Pierhill junction. Meadowbank stadium lies in this triangle, as did the former St Margarets shed.

At Craigentinny junction we enter the Portobello depot complex – named after Admiral Vernon's victory in 1739. To the north are a power station, a lighthouse and at Joppa there are saltpans. A goods line from Leith docks comes in through Baileyfield's engineering depot and the freightliner terminal, while to the south lie the carriage sidings and HST depots. The passenger line continues to Berwick, while we circle south on the goods line towards the extensive sidings at Millerhill yard beyond which lies Bilston Glen colliery. But we turn west at Niddrie West junction just before the brickworks and mine tips.

Just before the closed station of Duddington on the climb to Craigmiller, a line used to run to St Leonards. It passed Duddington loch and bird sanctuary, and the golf course below the 822 feet high Arthur's Seat to the north. A horseshoe curve takes us over the viaducts at Bridge End over Braid Burn with a fine view of the 14th century Craigmillar Castle to the southeast, and Liberton Tower. Then we climb through the closed stations of Newington and Blackford Hill. To the south rise the University, the Royal Observatory built in 1896 and a TV relay tower and police radio mast on the summit at 500 feet. The Pentland Hills lie behind.

After the former stations of Morningside Road and Craiglockhart, a spur connects with the ex-Caledonian line to Carstairs at Slateford station. We run underneath this line's double bridge, one fork joining the Glasgow line at Dalry junction, west of Haymarket, and the closed fork running to the former Caledonian terminus at Princes Street. At the former station at Gorgy, the junction takes us back onto the Glasgow line by the rugby ground, completing our circle.

33. Class 27 No 27203 waits to leave Glasgow Queen Street with the 1400 to Edinburgh on 4 September 1977.
    The Glasgow–Edinburgh Inter City service is now in the hands of Class 47s fitted for push and pull working. There is also a morning HST service from Queen Street to Kings Cross via Edinburgh Waverley. LES NIXON

These next two views were taken on the Edinburgh suburban circle line on the 27 April 1984, when No 60009 *Union of South Africa* ran a series of special trains to celebrate the centenary of the opening of the line

34. *Top left* No 60009 passes by the famous Braille School at Morningside in the south-western suburbs. JOHN LAVERICK

35. *Bottom left Union of South Africa* and empty stock are pictured at the end of the day winding round the freight only section near Blackford Hill as they head for Falkirk. DAVID EATWELL

36. *Top right Maude* leaves the eastern end of Calton tunnel (to the east of Waverley station) with a special on the circle route organised by McEwans Brewery to promote the Edinburgh Jazz Festival which is sponsored by that brewery. 5 June 1986.

37. *Bottom right* No 673 with the ECS for the above train hurries eastwards from Falkirk and is seen near Park Farm a mile to the east of Linlithgow.

38. *Top left* A pleasant reminder of when the mighty Deltics were the principal motive power on the East Coast main line as No 55004 *Queen's Own Highlander* heads out of Edinburgh Waverley with the 1150 to Kings Cross on a Spring day in the late 1970s.
TOM HEAVYSIDE

39. *Bottom left* LNER 4-4-0 *Morayshire* pulls through the eastern end of Waverley station on 11 May 1983 with the empty stock of a special train which is returning to Falkirk via Craigentinny and the Edinburgh suburban circle line. It will gain access to the Edinburgh–Falkirk–Glasgow main line at Haymarket West junction. The section from Craigentinny to this junction being now a goods only line. This route and the main line to Glasgow are former LNER (North British) lines.

The signal box and goods lines on the left of the picture have been demolished and taken up. The area is now a car park.

40. *Above* Another view of the eastern end of Waverley station taken on 11 May 1983 as an English Electric Class 37 is about to enter Calton Hill tunnel with a southbound tanker train.

The outer platforms of Waverley are through routes the inner ones being dead ends.

41, 42, 43 and 44. On 3 August 1975 LNER 4-4-0 No 246 *Morayshire* and Caledonian 0-4-4 tank No 419 left the headquarters of the SRPS at Falkirk with a special train for the 150 Celebrations at Darlington.

41 and 42. No 246 (upper) and No 419 (lower) are being prepared prior to their trip south.

43 and 44. The two beautiful locomotives and vintage stock are seen on the 1 in 100 climb out of Falkirk Grahamston as they head for Darlington via Edinburgh.

Between Polmont junction and Greenhill junction there are two routes through Falkirk, both used by Glasgow–Edinburgh trains. The upper route via Falkirk Grahamston connects with the Glasgow–Stirling line at Larbert junction.

45 and 46. Two notable visitors to Scotland on 7 April 1986 were 9F 2-10-0 *Evening Star* and LNER V2 2-6-2 *Green Arrow*. Both are pictured at Millerhill depot, Edinburgh, on the morning of the 7th prior to working to Haymarket coal depot. Later on that day they worked a special train from Waverley to Gleneagles.

47. *Top right* Bo'ness station 30 March 1986. Caledonian 0-4-4 tank pauses in the station after arriving with a late afternoon train from Kinneil. The Bo'ness and Kinneil Railway is situated on the southern shore of the river Forth. The line is now truncated but originally joined the Edinburgh–Falkirk line some two miles to the west of Linlithgow.

48. *Bottom right* The River Forth provides an attractive backcloth as No 419 does some evening shunting on the same day as the above picture.

Previous page
49. *Left* A smart looking Class 47/4 No 47407 in the new ScotRail livery threads its way out of Edinburgh Waverley on 30 March 1986 with the 1430 service to Glasgow Queen Street.

50. *Top right* Class 47/7 No 47702 *Saint Cuthbert* is seen just west of Greenhill junction heading for Edinburgh with the 1200 from Glasgow Queen Street.

The building on the right is part of the former goods shed at the junction, the station having been demolished some years ago. (See picture No 75).

Greenhill junction is where the two routes through Falkirk to Edinburgh split and is also the junction for the Glasgow–Stirling–Perth route.

51. *Bottom right* Class 37 No 37027, complete with Highland Terrier motif, poses at the SRPS depot at Falkirk after bringing in the empty stock for a special train. 11 May 1983.

52. *Above Morayshire* passes over the Forth Clyde canal some half a mile to the west of Falkirk Grahamston station 7 September 1980. D. J. O'ROURKE

53. *Top right* On 4 May 1980 *Maude* in charge of a special from Edinburgh to Falkirk crosses Linlithgow viaduct to the east of Polmont.

54. *Bottom right* Saturday 15 December 1985. The fourth (and last) Edinburgh circle trip of the day. North British 0-6-0 *Maude* and four coaches glow in the evening sun as they pass behind the famous Edinburgh landmark – Arthur's Seat. DAVID EATWELL

55. *Above* North British Railway 0-6-0 No 673 *Maude* passes
underneath Peffermill Road at Craigmiller on the Edinburgh
suburban line. 15 December 1985. BRIAN DOBBS

56. *Above* Class 37 No 37144 approaches
Carmuirs junction west on the evening of
11 May 1983 with a tank train from
Grangemouth Refinery bound for Glasgow
and the south. The line just visible in the
top right hand corner of the picture is the
main Glasgow–Stirling route.

57. *Right* Turning round from the previous
picture we see Class 20s No 20016 and
20220 leaving Carmuirs junction east and
heading for Glasgow on the same evening
with a mixed freight train. The line on the
left hand side of the picture meets the
Glasgow–Stirling line at Larbert junction (a
short distance to the north) thus forming a
triangle. Falkirk Grahamston station is just
over a mile to the east of this location.

Two scenes from BR steam days taken on Sunday 19 June 1966.

58. *Above* Class 5MT 4-6-0 No 45469 has just arrived at Platform 10 Waverley station with the 2.35 p.m. train from Carstairs. With the closure of the former LMS Princess Street station the previous year, all trains were then re-routed into Waverley. Note the Edinburgh shed code – 64C, and also the style of railway uniform, a far cry from today's outfits.

59. *Below* St Margarets shed Edinburgh with Gresley V2 2-6-2 No 60919 at rest. By the look of the smokebox door and buffers the locomotive had recently worked a 'special'. On the left is standard Class 4 2-6-4 tank No 80026. This locomotive was built in 1951 and withdrawn in September 1966.

SECTION THREE

GLASGOW — STIRLING — PERTH — DUNDEE — ABERDEEN

The Aberdeen train called the "St Mungo" after Glasgow's patron saint used to terminate at Buchanan Street station. When this closed, on 7 November 1966, the service changed to Queens Street. For this route description as far as Castle Cary, see Section Four.

For Stirling, we take the Falkirk Grahamston loop, but at Carmuirs West junction we turn north on the ex-Caledonian line, through Larbert junction and over the River Carron into Larbert station. An ICI depot lies to the left, as we pass the former spur to Denny to the west. There is a restriction of 70 mph as far as Dunblane. A rise of 1 in 126 takes us under two recent bridges linking the M8 and M9, then through the former Alloa junction, now Plean junction, where a short spur, formerly an Alloa branch, leads to Plean timber yard, then we run through the closed station of Plean.

After the former station at Bannockburn on a descent of 1 in 118, a junction takes a spur past the battlefield of 1314 to Polmaise colliery to the east. Ahead, Stirling Castle tops a great crag to the left, Cambuskenneth Abbey stands in a loop of the River Forth to the right and the gothic tower of the Wallace Monument rises on a hill beyond. We pass a spur on the right to a MOD installation. Stirling station boasts of a graceful roof to the concourse of hooped ribs springing from a central column. The platforms are decorated with flower tubs of tractor tyres painted Caledonian blue.

We cross the River Forth half a mile on near the original stone road bridge behind the new bridge on the left, while on the north bank on the right an ex-NB spur runs to Alloa yard, formerly to Dunfermline. We climb 1 in 100 past the sites of the rival companies' sheds and through Bridge of Allan station. We follow Allan Water up a narrow wooded valley with the Orchil Hills to the east, passing through Kippenross tunnel and emerging up 1 in 78 to reach Dunblane station. The cathedral across the river rises above banks of rhododendrons.

Immediately before the flat girder bridge over Allan Water, an ex-Caledonian line used to run west to Callander, Crianlarich and Oban. We climb 1 in 88 to Kinbuck's former station, where the gradient eases along Strath Allan. The old road crosses here but the new A9 built on General Wade's military road runs in a dead straight line beside us as far as Greenloaning station, now closed.

The line curves east through the former station at Blackford; the level crossing is for the old A9. A tight curve at the summit brings us to Gleneagles station

smartly painted in crimson and cream. The empty platform under the footbridge from the original ticket office served the closed branch to Crieff. We descend 1 in 100 north-east down Strath Earn. This is a very fast stretch through the former stations of Auchterarder, Dunning and Forteviot; the lonely box near Dunning has a monkey-puzzle tree.

Crossing the River Earn we see the viaduct of the Ladybank line which joins us from the right at Hilton junction. Moncrieffe tunnel takes us half a mile under the M90-M85 interchange and brings us past the sidings at Friarton by the prison. We run past St Leonard's Bridge with a good view of the Dundee line approaching over the Tay. This joins us south of Perth General station.

The ex-Caledonian Dundee line over the viaduct is single as far as the former Princess Street station. As the line turns south it skirts the sea cliff at the foot of Barnhill. The line is fairly level to Dundee and follows the north coast of the Tay eastwards through the former stations of Kinfauns and Glencarse, then through the raspberry fields of the Carse of Gowrie. Inchcoonans goods halt is closed but Errol station is still busy. Two miles to the north at Kinnaird, a railway was laid to a colliery using a batch of iron rails from Coalbrookdale dated 13 November 1767.

We pass a disused airfield and beyond it the sands of Dog Bank. At the closed station of Inchture a spur to the village inland, Longforgan station, is no more but Invergowrie, by the shore below the medical school, serves the west side of Dundee and gives a good view of Tay Bridge. After the former station at Ninewells, our line joins the ex-NB line at Buckingham junction. The former Caledonian terminal Dundee West and the sheds used to occupy the sidings up on our left as we run down below sea level to Dundee station (formerly NB Tay Bridge station).

We enter Dock Street tunnel under the approach to the new Tay Road bridge and emerge below the Old Town at Camperdown junction by the Blue Circle Cement depot. The line is the former Dundee and Arbroath Joint, and runs past docklands through the former Stannergate and West Ferry stations to Broughty Ferry where a spur runs to the pier. The closed Caledonian line to Forfar used to bridge the line here.

At Monifieth station the line cuts off Buddon Ness behind the Barry firing range. The station is closed but Barry Links, the new Golf Street and Carnoustie

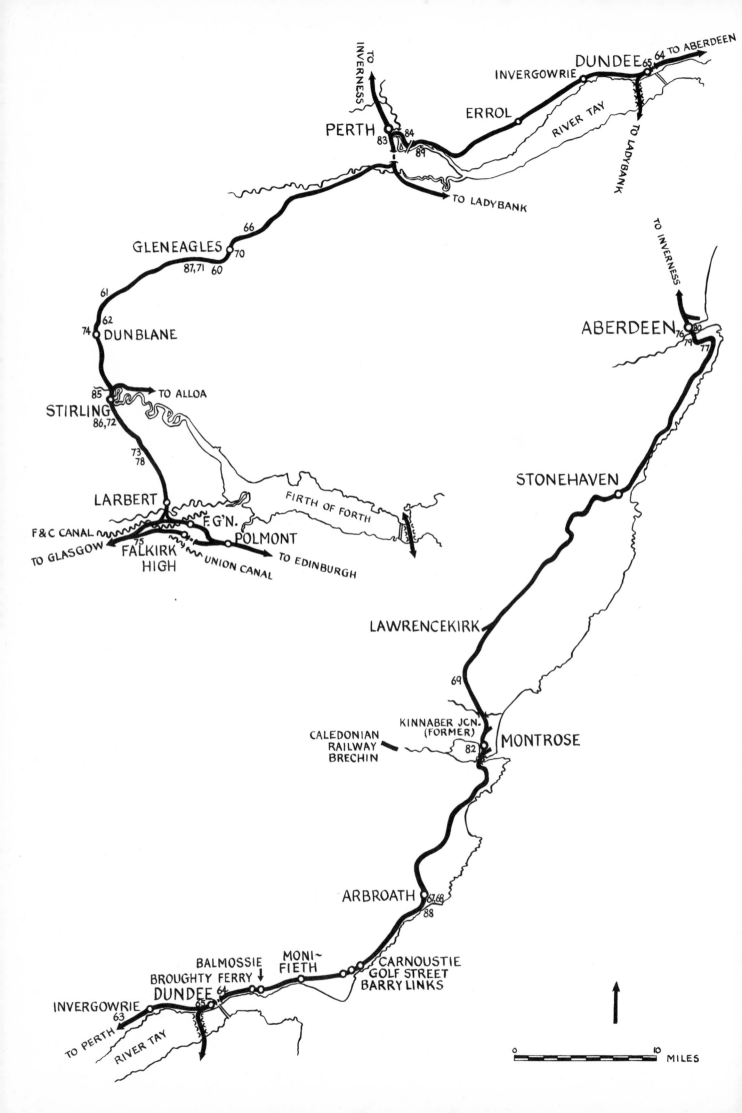

60. *Above* A reminder of the old days in Scotland as Gresley
Pacific No 60009 *Union of South Africa,* a regular performer on the
Glasgow–Aberdeen three hour expresses, is shown in action near
Gleneagles with an eight coach Edinburgh–Perth special on 13
April 1985. JOHN COOPER-SMITH

remain. The line hugs the rocky shore, through the
closed East Haven, past the disused airfield and golf
course, to Elliot junction where a spur at Wormiehills is
all that remains of the Carmyllie branch.

We run into Arbroath, famous for its smoked had-
dock which are prepared in a factory next to the station.
We run over a level crossing with a high box to St
Vigeans junction where a Caledonian line formerly ran
to Forfar, while our ex-NB line undulates through the
closed stations of Letham Grange, Inverkeilor and
Lunan Bay, dropping 1 in 111 past Usan box to
Montrose's mile-wide harbour, where a spur used to run
right to Ferryden dock. Montrose is famous for its two
viaducts, the south one of red brick arches, the north of
flat girders.

At the north end after the station, a NB branch used
to run to Bervie on the coast and a Caledonian line used
to pass under us to Forfar; Brechin station and a section
of line is now preserved. We climb 1 in 90, through the
closed station at Hillside with its distillery spur, to the
former Kinnaber junction. The Caledonian line from

Stanley junction used to join here. We drop through
Craigo and rise 1 in 104 through Marykirk and Lawrence-
kirk, all closed. A goods spur runs west, then the line
drops to Fordoun, closed, and rises to the summit at the
former station at Drumlithie. Newmill siding lies where
the line snakes to Carmont, also closed, then the line
drops 1 in 92 to Stonehaven station.

We rise to follow the cliff edge through the closed
stations of Muchalls and Newtonhill, over the girder
viaduct over the Burn of Elsick, then through Portleven
and Cove Bay, also closed. We make reverse curves west
and north, between the former shed and Torry headland, and cross the River Dee, whose banks are host to
golden daffodils.

On the north side is Ferryhill yard. At its junction the
GN of S line used to come in from Boat of Garten. Just
before Aberdeen station, spurs run to the docks on the
right. The station is being refurbished, with glass walls
and staircases painted red, making a colourful setting
for the blue-and-silver livery of the ScotRail stock.

61. *Top left Green Arrow* and *Evening Star* are pictured at Kinbuck on 7 April 1986 with the EMI special train from Edinburgh–Gleneagles (the train originated at Kings Cross).

Kinbuck is the summit of Dunblane bank which starts just north of Stirling and runs for six miles at around 1 in 100 the steepest gradient being 1 in 78.

This line is part of the original Caledonian Railway route to Aberdeen via Perth, Stanley junction and Kinnaber junction. The latter junction being where the Caledonian and North British Railways met, much featured in the famous West coast and East coast race to the North in the 1890s.

Stanley junction to Kinnaber was closed some years ago, the

main route from Glasgow to Aberdeen now being via Perth and Dundee.

62. *Bottom left* An Edinburgh–Aberdeen special hauled by No 60009 is caught by the camera just north of Dunblane on 18 April 1981.

63. *Above Union of South Africa* makes a fine sight as it speeds along the line near Invergowrie on 9 May 1981 with the *North Briton* from Glasgow to Dundee and then Edinburgh via Tay and Forth bridges. CHRIS MILNER

64. *Above* On a very wet Saturday, 1 October 1983, *Union of South Africa* in charge of an Edinburgh–Aberdeen special train blasts its way out of Dundee up the 1 in 60 to Camperdown junction. DAVID WILCOCK

65. *Top right* On the same day as the previous picture No 60009 approaches Dundee station on its journey to Aberdeen. Note the fine semaphore signals which have all since been replaced by colour light signalling and the signal box has also been removed.

Dundee at one time had two major stations, Dundee West and the present station which was then called Dundee Tay Bridge. West

was the Caledonian station for the line from Perth and Tay Bridge the North British station for the route from Edinburgh. Finally note the steep gradient (1 in 66) down into the station
JOHN LAVERICK

66. *Bottom right* On a very dull 1 October 1983 LNER Pacific No 4472 *Flying Scotsman* makes a pleasing sight as it heads for Perth with the *Fair Maid* from Glasgow (Moss End) to Perth and then via Ladybank to Edinburgh. The location is Auchterarder, two miles north west of Gleneagles. CHRIS MILNER

67. *Left* Class 47/7 No 47704 *Dunedin* approaches Arbroath on 2 April 1986 with the 1125 Glasgow Queen Street–Aberdeen service.

68. *Below* Arbroath still boasts a very fine station (as indeed do many Scottish towns and cities). In this view of the station on 2 April 1986 we see Class 47/4 No 47408 arriving with the 1200 Aberdeen–Edinburgh service. Just above the station name is the date it was built – 1911. Arbroath is situated on the east coast and is a well known fishing town famous for its smoked fish.

69. *Top right* Class 47/7 No 47712 *Lady Diana Spencer* hurries through Craigo, some two miles to the north of the former junction at Kinnaber, on the evening of 2 April 1986 with the 1525 Glasgow–Aberdeen service.

70. *Below* It is early afternoon at Gleneagles station on 1 April 1986 as Class 47/4 No 47636 arrives with the up *Clansman*, the 1030 Inverness–Birmingham New Street.

Gleneagles was once the junction for the branch to Crieff to the north west.

Also at Gleneagles is the world famous Gleneagles Hotel once owned by the London Midland and Scottish Railway.

71. *Above* The *EMI Music Express* from Edinburgh to Gleneagles with No 4771 and No 92220 in charge races along the level section at Blackford some two miles to the south of its destination. 7 April 1986. Note the fine semaphore signal complete with Caledonian type post.

72. *Below* On a beautiful Spring evening, 12 April 1984, Class 5MT No 44767 *George Stephenson* heads south out of Stirling with a return Perth–Falkirk special following the BR open day at Perth. LES NIXON

73. *Above* No 60009 storms up the 1 in 126 near Plean Junction (south of Stirling) with an Edinburgh–Aberdeen special on 18 April 1981.

74. *Below* No 44767 climbs through the neat station at Dunblane with a Falkirk–Perth special on 13 April 1985.
The station is located halfway up Dunblane bank which is situated just north of Stirling and the summit is at Kinbuck.
JOHN COOPER-SMITH

Memories of BR steam days on the Glasgow–Aberdeen route are shown in the next four pictures.

75. *Top left* Ex WD 2-8-0 No 90071 trundles through the station at Greenhill junction with a train of empty coal wagons from the Glasgow area probably bound for the Fife coalfields via Alloa Junction. 18 June 1966.

Part of the goods sidings and sheds can be seen at the back of the train. (See Section Two picture No 50).

76. *Bottom left* LNER A4 Pacific No 60034 *Lord Faringdon* is serviced at Aberdeen Ferryhill shed on 14 June 1966 prior to working the 1.30 p.m. Aberdeen–Glasgow, the *Grampian*. Note the non-corridor tender.

77. *Top right* A4 Pacific No 60019 *Bittern* is seen climbing the steep grade up to Cove Bay with the 5.15 p.m. Aberdeen-Glasgow train. 14 June 1966. The city of Aberdeen is in the background.

78. *Bottom right* LNER A2 Pacific No 60532 *Blue Peter* speeds along near Plean junction with the 1.30 p.m. Aberdeen Glasgow train on 18 June 1966. No 60532 together with No 60530 *Sayajirao* were the last two of this very powerful class of locomotives to be in service. Happily *Blue Peter* is preserved and can be seen at Dinting Railway Centre.

79. Next page A fine action picture of No 60009 as it leaves Aberdeen on 14 April 1979 with a return special to Edinburgh. Aberdeen's famous gantries have sadly all been replaced by colour light signalling. LES NIXON

80. *Left* Sunshine and shadows at Aberdeen station on 3 April 1986 as Class 08 No 08680 shunts empty coaching stock.

The train leaving on the left is the 1105 service to Glasgow. As well as trains to the south there is still a regular passenger service from Aberdeen to Elgin and Inverness in the north west, part of the Great North of Scotland route which joined with the Highland Railway at Elgin for the remaining 54 miles to Inverness. This route from Aberdeen to Inverness is extremely attractive with some very fine scenery and many interesting stations; there are also quite a lot of freight workings on this route.

81. *Below* Class 47/4 No 47472 passes Cadder signal box between Bishopbriggs and Lenzie on the Glasgow–Edinburgh main line (see map, section two) with the 0925 Glasgow–Aberdeen train on 5 September 1983. The line to Aberdeen branches off at Greenhill junction. TOM NOBLE

82. *Above* Class 40 No 40158 arrives at Montrose (on the east coast) with the 1925 Aberdeen–Kings Cross train on 11 May 1977. TOM HEAVYSIDE

83. *Below* Another Class 40, this time No 40065 arrives at the Dundee line platforms at Perth on 20 May 1978 with a southbound empty stock train. TOM HEAVYSIDE

84. *Above* Crossing the River Tay at Perth on 19 April 1981 is 4-4-0 No 246 in charge of a special bound for Dundee. The new bridge on the right makes a contrast with the older bridge on the left which was built by Telford.

85. *Left* 4-6-0 No 44767 crosses the River Forth at Stirling with a return excursion from the BR open day at Perth to Edinburgh. 13 April 1985.
BRIAN DOBBS

86. *Top right* For the present Stirling still boasts many fine old semaphore signals as can be seen in this view of Class 37 No 37405 pulling through the station on 31 March 1986 with a southbound empty stock train.

Note the new style livery complete with Highland Terrier.

87. *Bottom right* Storm clouds gather over the Perthshire hills as No 44767 hurries through Blackford with an Edinburgh–Perth special train. 13 April 1985. BRIAN DOBBS

88. *Above* Union of South Africa heads round the coast at Arbroath with an Edinburgh–Aberdeen special on 14 April 1979. LES NIXON

89. *Right* Class D49 No 246 *Morayshire* on a Perth-Dundee special at Kinfauns just east of Perth. 19 April 1981.
   Note the 'ruined' castle at the top of the picture. These were built around this part of the River Tay because this area was supposed to resemble parts of the Rhine. The 'ruins' being built to further this illusion. JOHN COOPER-SMITH

SECTION FOUR

EDINBURGH — LADYBANK — PERTH/DUNDEE

EDINBURGH — LADYBANK — PERTH/DUNDEE

We leave Edinburgh Waverley and run west through Haymarket as described in Section Two, passing the coal depot on the right and a distillery on the left. We fork right and head north through the former station at Turnhouse near the airport, then through the former Dalmeny South junction where the closed line from Ratho joined in. We climb 1 in 100 to Dalmeny North junction by a tank farm where a goods line comes in from Falkirk, and a former line came up from South Queensferry pier.

At Dalmeny station we see the Forth Bridge with the road suspension bridge to the west, completed in 1964. The rail bridge is of cantilever construction, designed by Sir Benjamin Baker and built by William Arrol. It was opened on 14 March 1840. The total length is 5,350 feet of double track, with a high water clearance of 150 feet. The three main piers each support two cantilever arms 680 feet long with 350 feet suspended spans between the ends. The towers are 361 feet high. It used 54,000 tons of Siemen-Martin open-hearth steel, stronger than mild steel, which was produced in workshops at South Queensferry. Much of the structure is of rolled steel girders but the biggest compression members are 12 foot diameter tubes of riveted plates. Baker calculated for a wind pressure of 56 lbs per square inch, compared with the 10 lbs of the first Tay bridge.

At North Queensferry station, a spur runs underneath to the naval base at Rosyth. Our line drops down 1 in 70 through two tunnels to Inverkeithing. The station has recently been reconstructed in a "Neo-Palladian" style. To the right is a spur to James White's shipbreakers yard. At Central junction on the north side of the station the line forks, the east line goes to Burntisland and the west to Cowdenbeath. The first turns through Inverkeithing East junction, rises 1 in 94¼ to Dalgety box then drops 1 in 100 to meet the coast at Aberdour station above the castle and harbour of Sir Patrick Spens' fame. It continues down to Burntisland station and shipyard and follows the edge of the mile-wide sands to Kinghorn tunnel and station. A steady rise inland passes the spur to Moss Morran liquid gas depot and Braefoot tanker terminal near the Seafield tower. After Kirkcaldy station there is a goods spur on the left, and after Sinclair station two spurs connect with a works on the left. A rise of 1 in 100 takes us through the closed station at Dysart and the summit, then descends to Thornton junction with a speed restriction due to colliery subsidence.

The west fork, from Inverkeithing North junction, climbs steeply through coalfields at Rosyth halt to Dunfirmline Lower station, approaching it via Charlestown junction. A goods line runs west to Stirling, but the Longannet to Alloa section is now out of use. A spur off this line drops from Elbowend junction down to Crombie. Nearby, the 5th Earl of Elgin built his Charlestown railway in 1767 from his coalpits near Dunfermline to the Firth near Rosyth. This also carried passengers for the Granton-Stirling packets.

Dunfermline is an ancient seat of kings; 15 are buried here in the Abbey including Robert the Bruce. The steel baron Andrew Carnegie was born here and his Trust founded in 1903 has created benefits such as the Pittencrieff Glen park.

The locomotive shed used to lie northwest of the station. At Townhill yard a line comes in from the Rexco coking plant to the west. We climb past through the side of Halbeath station, up 1 in 100 to Cowdenbeath New station, where the Glenfarg route used to run north. We drop through Lochgelly and Cardenden stations between which a spur runs north to Bowhill works from Glencraig junction. The rest of this route past Thornton yard is a goods line, meeting the first route at the Thornton North junction.

Opposite, a branch runs east to Cameron Bridge distilleries and Leven and Methil docks – the remains of the Fife coastal route via St Andrews. The private railway from Lochty to Knightswood is the terminus of an inland spur. Our line continues to Markinch station; on the left is the Co-op coal depot and the Auchmuty spur supplying the Tullis Russel paper company near Glenrothes, a new colliery and electronics town established in 1950, and Fife airport.

We climb 1 in 102 to the summit of Lochmuir Box and descend 1 in 105 through the former Falkland Road station, for the palace. We run down through Kingskettle at 1 in 95 to reach Ladybank station and junction.

Gentle gradients take our passenger line northeast through Springfield station and to Cupar, the royal burgh and capital of Fife. A mile south of the station stands the great tower of the 16th century Scotstarvit mansion. Another rise through the closed station at Dairsie and fall takes us to Leuchars junction and station by the harbour and airfield. The coastal route used to rejoin just south of here. The Tayport coastal loop ahead is now closed.

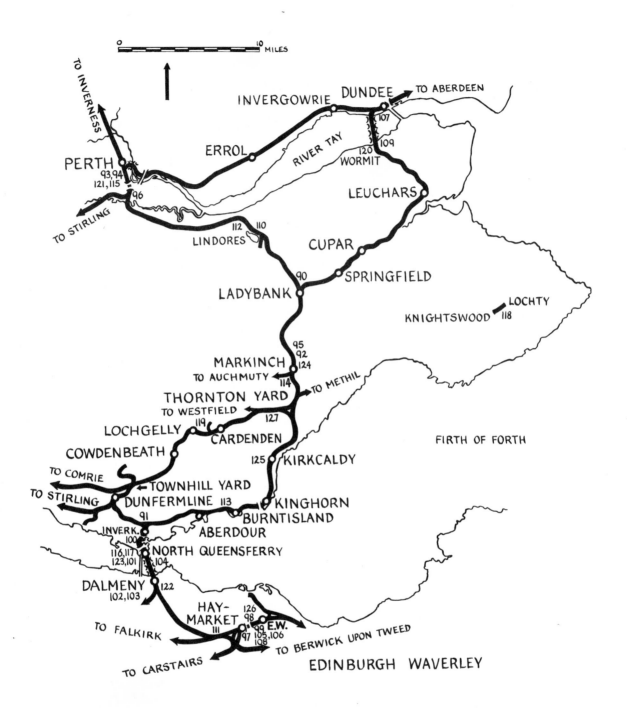

We rise through the former station at St Fort where the closed line from Lindores used to join from the west, then we drop through the former goods yard at Wormit on the south bank of the Tay. The present Tay bridge built by William Arrol replaces the one which collapsed in the December gale of 1879 with the Edinburgh mail. The piers still show on the east side. The present viaduct is a series of flat girder spans carrying two tracks with a tight curve at the northern end. We run through the site of Esplanade station and follow the shore past extensive sidings and former sheds into Dundee station, the former NB Tay Bridge station. The elegant new road bridge rises over us just beyond.

From Ladybank by the northwest line we follow the single track through the former station at Collessie where Clatchard Craig have a spur. At Glenburnie, a line via St Fort used to link up with Leuchars. We turn west along the Tay's south shore through the sites of Newburgh and Abernethy stations, and past Balmano junction with the former Glenfarg line which was closed on 5 January 1970. Just after the former Bridge of Earn station, our line meets the ex-Caledonian line from Stirling, and at Hilton junction the line becomes double again as we run into Perth station.

△1

1. No 5407 leaves Mallaig on Sunday 14 July 1985 with the 1800 to Fort William. This is indeed a rare picture because, apart from a few days in the summer of 1985, all locomotives have faced Mallaig, resulting in tender-first workings to Fort William.
ROGER HILL

Next pages

2. Caledonian 0-4-4 tank No 419 at Bo'ness. 30 March 1986.
CHRISTINA SIVITER

3. *Union of South Africa* poses at Larbert on the morning of 27 April 1985 prior to working a special from Falkirk to Edinburgh.
DAVID EATWELL

4. *Morayshire* leaves the Tay Bridge at Wormit and heads for Falkirk with a special from Dundee. 19 April 1981.
CHRISTINA SIVITER

5. *The Royal Scotsman* hauled by 44767 heads for Mallaig on the morning of 31 May 1985 and is seen near Banavie crossing.
ROGER HILL

△4 5▽

previous pages

6. The picturesque station of Kyle of Lochalsh is the setting as Class 37 No 37025 waits to leave for Inverness with a return special working. The Isle of Skye dominates the background. 5 October 1982.

7. Class 47 No 47408 leaves Edinburgh Waverley with the 1320 to Dundee on 30 March 1986.

8. *Flying Scotsman* is dwarfed by the Forth Bridge as it heads south on 1 October 1983 with a train from Perth.

9. North Queensferry is the location as *Morayshire* heads south with a special excursion on 11 May 1983. JOHN LAVERICK

above

10. *Maude* crosses Nan-Uamh viaduct on 28 May 1984 with the SLOA West Highlander special from Fort William to Arisaig. JOHN COOPER-SMITH

opposite

11. No 60009 crosses the Tay at Perth with an Edinburgh–Aberdeen train. 18 April 1981.

12. The sun is setting as No 47467 passes Welshs Bridge box Inverness with the 1540 Aberdeen–Inverness train. 4 April 1986. CHRISTINA SIVITER

13△ △14

13. Slochd viaduct is the setting as Nos 37021 and 47205 doublehead the 1430 Inverness–Perth train. 4 April 1986. CHRISTINA SIVITER

14. *Maude* at Waverley with a special train on 5 June 1986.

15. No 47551 pulls out of Stirling with the 1030 Inverness–Birmingham train. 31 March 1986.

△15

90. *Above* Gresley 4-4-0 Class D49 No 246 *Morayshire* makes a
fine sight as it heads out of Ladybank on the 19 April 1981 with a
Falkirk–Ladybank–Perth special. LES NIXON

91. *Above* No 246 approaches
Inverkeithing station on a very wet
11 May 1983 with the empty stock
for a return special to Edinburgh.
The train is coming in on the line
from Rosyth and Dunfermline. The
line from Dunfermline to Thornton
Junction is still open for goods traffic
only.

 The line on the right of the picture
is the main line to Dundee via
Thornton Junction and Ladybank.
Ladybank is the junction for the
single line section to Perth.

92. *Left* On 1 October 1983 A4
Pacific No 60009 climbs the stiff
grades out of Markinch with the
Aberdonian from Edinburgh to
Dundee via the Forth and Tay
bridges.

93 and 94. On the same day as the previous picture *Flying Scotsman* was in charge of the *Fair Maid* ten coach special train from Glasgow (Moss End) to Perth via Stirling.

In the upper picture the special is seen approaching Perth and passing by the goods yard just to the south of the station. In the lower scene we see the special entering Perth station. *Flying Scotsman* will then leave its train to be turned on the turntable in readiness for the return journey south. The Dundee line platforms are on the extreme righthand side of the picture. The platforms in the middle are used by the Highland line trains to and from Inverness and the remainder for specials and freight movements.

95. *Above* No 246 climbs the 1 in 102 out of Markinch with a Falkirk–Ladybank–Dundee train. After reversing at Dundee the train then ran to Perth and back before returning to Falkirk via the 'bridges' route. 19 April 1981.

These fine looking 4-4-0 locomotives were introduced in 1927 and designed by Sir Nigel Gresley. Sadly this is the only surviving member of this once numerous class.

96. *Right* Another view of *Morayshire* on 19 April 1981. This time as it leaves Hilton Junction, just south of Perth, and heads for that fair city with the special from Falkirk.

The line on the left that the train is entering from is from Ladybank and the line on the right is the direct route to Glasgow and Edinburgh via Stirling, Edinburgh trains gaining the main Glasgow–Edinburgh line via Larbert Junction and Polmont and Glasgow trains joining the same line at Greenhill Junction.

The old North British route from Perth to Edinburgh via Bridge of Earn (on the Ladybank line) and Kinross Junction to Cowdenbeath was closed many years ago. This was also popularly known as the Glenfarg route. Happily this picturesque route has been preserved in print through the many fine photographs of one of the leading railway photographers of our time – W. J. V. Anderson. Ironically the M90 motorway from Perth–Edinburgh runs for part of the way on the trackbed of this route.
JOHN COOPER-SMITH

Next page
97, 98, 99 and 100. On 4 May 1980 veteran 0-6-0 No 673 *Maude* ran a series of excursions from Edinburgh to Inverkeithing. This fine old North British Railway locomotive was built in the late 1880s to a design by Holmes and ran on BR until the mid 1960s. Happily for us it was preserved by the Scottish Railway Preservation Society at Falkirk and as can be seen from this book makes frequent trips on the BR main line.

97. *Top left* No 673 gives off a fine exhaust as it runs through Haymarket on the outskirts of Edinburgh and heads for Inverkeithing. LES NIXON

98. *Bottom left Maude* pulls out of Waverley with an afternoon train for Inverkeithing.

99. *Top right* Princess Street Gardens provide an attractive setting for *Maude* as it hurries out of Edinburgh with one of the excursions for Inverkeithing.

100. *Bottom right* The veteran 0-6-0 climbs the 1 in 70 from Inverkeithing to North Queensferry with a return excursion to Edinburgh.

101. *Above* The small town of North Queensferry nestles below
the northern approach section of the Forth Bridge as A3 Pacific No
4472 *Flying Scotsman* makes steady progress with a Perth–
Edinburgh special on the evening of 1 October 1983.

102. *Top left* On 11 May 1983 No 246 is seen at the northern end of the Forth Bridge with a special train to Rosyth Dockyards. This bridge which is almost two miles in length must surely be one of the most beautiful ever built.

103. *Bottom left* This view taken from North Queensferry shows *Maude* with an Edinburgh–Inverkeithing special on 4 May 1980. South Queensferry can be clearly seen in the background.
LES NIXON

104. *Above* The Forth Bridge was once called 'The Cathedral of Steam' and in this view of No 60009 with the *Forth Bridge Flyer* running beneath its girders on 25 May 1985 it is easy to see why.
DAVID WILCOCK

105. *Top left* Class 47/4 No 47463 threads the line through Princess Street Gardens on Sunday 6 April 1986 with the 1030 Dundee–Edinburgh train.

106. *Bottom left* The 1320 to Dundee hauled by Class 27 No 27707 heads out of Waverley station on 6 April 1986 and approaches the Mound tunnel at the start of its 59 mile journey via the Forth and Tay bridges.

107. *Top right* Class 26 No 26042 shunts the empty stock of the 1040 arrival from Edinburgh at Dundee station on 2 April 1986. This station was originally called Tay Bridge station. Dundee West which was closed some years ago was situated to the left of the picture.

108. *Bottom right* The North British hotel dominates Edinburgh Waverley station as Class 27 No 27036 pulls out on the evening of 10 May 1983 with a train for Dundee. The Class 47 is No 47710.

Next page
109. *Top left* The 'other' famous railway bridge in Scotland is the Tay Bridge. This bridge which is two miles in length crosses the Tay between Dundee and Wormit in the south.

This view of the southern end of the bridge shows *Morayshire* with a Dundee–Falkirk special on 19 April 1981. After the Tay Bridge disaster at the end of the last century the bridge was completely rebuilt but the base of the piers of the old bridge can still be seen in the right hand foreground of the picture TOM HEAVYSIDE

110. *Bottom left* *Morayshire* is admired from across Lindores Loch (near Newburgh between Perth and Ladybank) as the Gresley 4-4-0 returns the *Taysider* to Falkirk after travelling out via Edinburgh and Dundee. 7 September 1980.
DAVID EATWELL

111. *Top right* *Green Arrow* and *Evening Star* are seen at the western end of Waverley station heading for Haymarket coal depot. 7 April 1986. It must be nearly twenty years since a V2 or a 9F locomotive worked in Scotland. Unlike 9Fs, V2s were a common sight in Scotland in BR steam days but a combination of the two double heading would have been a rarity.

112. *Bottom right* *Flying Scotsman* moves sedately along the single line section between Hilton Junction and Ladybank with a Perth-Edinburgh excursion. 1 October 1983. The location is Newburgh. LES NIXON

113. *Above* A Perth–Edinburgh special hauled by 4472 skirts the Fife coastline at Burntisland on 1 October 1983. D. J. O'ROURKE

114. *Top right* *Maude* pauses for a photographic stop at Markinch and the SRPS crew members take the opportunity to shovel coal down the tender for the last leg of the journey from Perth to Falkirk. 15 October 1983. CHRIS MILNER

115. *Bottom right* The same train as in the previous picture only this time at Perth prior to departure for the return trip to Falkirk. DAVID EATWELL

118. *Above* 0-6-0 saddle tank No 16 of the Lochty Private Railway at work on June 13 1982. This line is situated near to Crail in Fife and runs between Knightswood and Lochty. Lochty was the terminus of the North British line from Cameron Bridge and Thornton Junction. DAVID WILCOCK

119. *Below Maude* in charge of a Perth–Falkirk special via Ladybank, Thornton Junction and Dunfermline is photographed near Lochgelly on 15 October 1983. The section between Thornton Junction and Cardenden is normally only used by goods traffic. JOHN LAVERICK

16. *Top left Morayshire* glows in ┊e evening sun as it leaves the rock ┊tting at North Queensferry and ┊ads for the Forth Bridge with a ┊uthbound special on 7 September ┊80. D. J. O'ROURKE

17. *Bottom left Union of South ┊frica* with a southbound special ┊imbs up to North Queensferry on ┊7 April 1985.

The famous Gresley A4 Pacific ┊comotives were first introduced in ┊35 for work on the East Coast Main ┊ne between Kings Cross and ┊dinburgh. They were displaced ┊om this work by the Deltic ┊comotives at the beginning of the ┊960s and finished up their days on ┊e tightly scheduled Glasgow–┊berdeen three hour expresses. ┊ortunately there are six examples of ┊is class preserved including *Mallard* ┊e holder of the world speed record ┊r steam traction – 126 miles per ┊our. This locomotive has been ┊stored to working order and is now ┊nning on special trains. ┊HN LAVERICK

120. *Above* On 6 September 1980 No 60009 rounds a curve near Wormit with an Edinburgh–Aberdeen special working.

121. *Top right* No 4472 accelerates out of Perth with a special to Edinburgh via Ladybank. 1 October 1983.

122. *Bottom right* On 14 April 1979 No 60009 approaches Dalmeny (just south of the Forth Bridge) with an Edinburgh–Aberdeen excursion.

123. *Left* The *Taysider* hauled by No 246 climbs through the cutting at North Queensferry as it heads south for Edinburgh. 7 September 1980.

124. *Above* On 19 April 1981 *Morayshire* is shown at Markinch heading northwards for Perth. Originally No 60009 was to have taken over the train at Markinch but unfortunately it 'threw' its centre big-end the day before at Aberdeen. DAVID EATWELL

125. *Below* Another shot of No 246 on 19 April 1981, this time as the Falkirk special leaves Kirkcaldy. TOM HEAVYSIDE

Previous pages
126. A close-up of North British 0-6-0 No 673 *Maude* as it leaves
Edinburgh on 4 May 1980 with an excursion to Inverkeithing.

127. *Above* Finally to finish this section a scene from the past in
Fife as Gresley Class J38 0-6-0 No 65914 trundles down the grade
towards Thornton Junction with a coal train from the
Cowdenbeath area. The location is Bowhill between Lochgelly and
Thornton and the date 16 June 1966.

This sturdy class of locomotive which was introduced in 1926
was mainly used on goods workings and with its 4′ 8″ driving
wheels and 28,415 lb tractive effort was capable of hauling heavy
loads. The Class J39 although very similar in appearance had
larger driving wheels (5′ 2″) and was primarily designed for
passenger work.

SECTION FIVE

PERTH — AVIEMORE — INVERNESS
(HIGHLAND MAIN LINE)

Our line heads north between Victoria Bridge over the River Tay and the spire of St John's, with its ancient peal of bells. This former Caledonian line passes goods sidings on the right for Shell and Dewars, and the turntable, and follows the river north. The semaphores went in the resignalling in 1965. At the bridge over the River Almond we see Scone Palace across the Tay, the ancient seat of the Kingdom. A Caledonian line formerly branched west to Crieff. We climb at 1 in 153 through the former stations of Luncarty and Strathford with its spur to Bankfoot now closed, and up 1 in 125 to Stanley junction. Here our line takes the left fork, the former Highland Railway line, but the ex-Caledonian line which went straight ahead to Kinnaber junction near Montrose has now been lifted.

The single track rises 1 in 80 over the level crossing at Murthley, now closed, and climbs 1 in 82 following the wooded pass under Rohallion Castle and King's Seat on Birnham Hill, then runs through Kingswood tunnel. The line snakes down 1 in 80 into the station and passing loop at Dunkeld. On departure, we cross the Falls of the Braan and have a good view of the famous cathedral across the Tay to the right.

After Inver tunnel we bend northwards. Between the closed stations of Dalguise and Guay we cross the Tay. At the confluence of River Tummel we follow it to the former station at Ballinluig, where there is a loop. Just before this, there used to be a branch to Aberfeldy on the left from the junction at Logierait, with two bridges at the meeting of the waters. At Moulinearn, the new bypass round Pitlochry crosses the river to our left as we climb 1 in 90 over the A9 to Pitlochry station and loop at 28 miles.

We now follow the River Garry leaving the River Tummel to the west. We climb 1 in 85 up the strategic Pass of Killiecrankie. We run under the A9 at Garry Bridge and hug the hillside on viaducts with picturesque crenellations on the parapets. The mountain Ben Vrackie rises to the northeast. Dropping slightly we run through Killiecrankie tunnel to the former station of Killiecrankie. To the left is "Soldier's Leap" over the narrows of the gorge. We rise wedged between road and river, at the top we cross the River Tilt on a bridge like a fortified castle, and reach Blair Atholl station. From here to Dalwhinnie the line is double track. Blair Castle is set back on the right and behind it rises the great mountain Beinn Dearg. We climb west up 1 in 80 up a wooded pass to cross the river Bruar just below the Falls.

At 40 miles we pass through the former station at Struan. Bankers were needed where the line steepens to 1 in 70 on the long drag. We cross to the south side of the river while General Wade's military road keeps to the north side. The next station at Dalnaspidal is now closed. Our line passes the north end of Loch Garry, then a haul up 1 in 78 takes us up to Druimachdar summit, at 1,484 feet the highest in the country; the up line here is controlled by Dalwhinnie and the down line by Blair. The 53 mile post lies by the border between Perthshire and Invernesshire.

On the descent, Loch Ericht to the west sends an aquaduct under the line to a power station on the east side. We run down 1 in 80 to Dalwhinnie station where the line becomes single track again. There is a distillery on the right. We follow the River Truim and its Falls on the left down 1 in 100 through open moorland. The Wade road takes the Corrieyairack pass, 2,507 feet high, on the left.

Coming down the 1 in 95 through Etteridge towards the Monadhliath mountains, we meet the confluence of the River Spey. We run into Newtonmore station. A low wooden viaduct nearby imposes a restriction of 65 mph. We continue our gentle descent through Kingussie station and its loop at 71½ miles, near Ruthven barracks to the east. Between here and Aviemore, HSTs may reach 100 mph. A slight rise brings us to Kincraig, now closed, and its loop, near the Highland Wildlife Park.

As we run down into the station at the ski resort at Aviemore, to the right we see the spectacular range of the Cairngorm mountains. Up trains generally use the down platform of the loop to save passengers having to use the footbridge. By the station is the terminus of the private Strathspey Railway that runs east to the Boat of Garten, formerly the HR line to Forres.

We begin the long climb to Slochd, rising 1 in 75 past the Craigellachie Nature reserve on the left. We reach Carrbridge where two picturesque humpbacked footbridges were built for carrying coffins. We run over Slochd viaduct over the River Dulnain, then up the 1 in 60 to the summit loop at 1,315 feet by the radio control mast.

We drop down 1 in 60 from the 95 mile post, through the treeless moors of Strath Dearn. Just before the loop at the former station at Tomatin, we cross the River Findhorn on a great viaduct of masonry and steel. It is 1,235 feet long, runs 140 feet above the river bed and curves on a radius of half a mile. We continue descen-

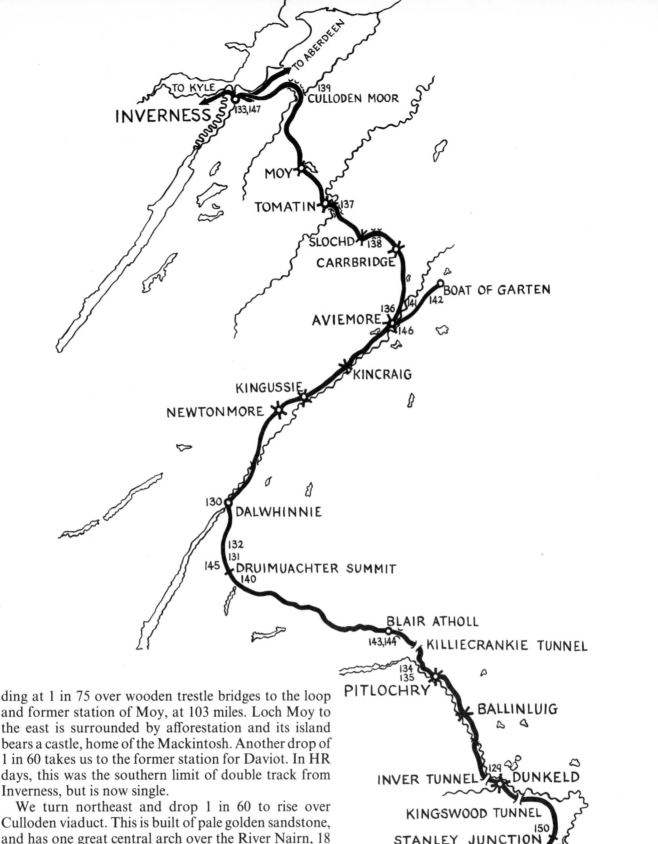

TO ABERDEEN
TO KYLE
139
CULLODEN MOOR
INVERNESS 133,147
MOY
TOMATIN 137
SLOCHD 138
CARRBRIDGE
141 BOAT OF GARTEN
136 142
AVIEMORE 146
KINCRAIG
KINGUSSIE
NEWTONMORE
130 DALWHINNIE
132
131
145 DRUIMUACHTER SUMMIT
140
BLAIR ATHOLL
143,144 KILLIECRANKIE TUNNEL
134
135
PITLOCHRY
BALLINLUIG
129
INVER TUNNEL DUNKELD
KINGSWOOD TUNNEL
STANLEY JUNCTION 150
(FORMER)
151
148,149
PERTH
128
TO DUNDEE
TO STIRLING
TO FORTH BRIDGE

0   10
                         MILES

ding at 1 in 75 over wooden trestle bridges to the loop
and former station of Moy, at 103 miles. Loch Moy to
the east is surrounded by afforestation and its island
bears a castle, home of the Mackintosh. Another drop of
1 in 60 takes us to the former station for Daviot. In HR
days, this was the southern limit of double track from
Inverness, but is now single.

We turn northeast and drop 1 in 60 to rise over
Culloden viaduct. This is built of pale golden sandstone,
and has one great central arch over the River Nairn, 18
smaller ones to the south and 10 to the north. We pass a
spur after this to the Highlands Bitumen Co at
Newlands. Our line becomes double again and we curve
round over Culloden Moor, the scene of the Jacobite
defeat in 1745. We drop down 1 in 60 to cross over the
Aberdeen line and we join it at Millburn junction.

Inverness station, at 118 miles, has sidings for the
cement terminal on the right, near a former shed.
Another shed lay on the left. Originally the line
approached the station by a stone water tower in the
shape of a great triumphal arch. The triangle of the
terminal used to enclose the HR Lochgorm locomotive
works, now a diesel depot.

128. *Above* On Monday 20 July 1981 Class 5MT No 5025 sets out from Perth with the *Speyside Express* bound for Aviemore a distance of some 83 miles. DAVID EATWELL

129. *Below* In glorious evening sunshine the return *Speyside Express* is caught by the camera as it climbs the 1 in 300 grade up to Inver tunnel, Dunkeld. 20 July 1981.

   The Black 5 locomotive, whose home is on the Strathspey Railway, was turned on the former Kyle of Lockalsh turntable now installed at the Strathspey Railway's Aviemore depot. DAVID EATWELL

130. *Above* The *Osprey Express* from Edinburgh–Aviemore with No 60009 in charge is seen hurrying northwards past Buchanan's Distillery at Dalwhinnie on 25 August 1980. This distillery is the home of Dalwhinnie Malt Whisky.
LES NIXON

131. *Below* The weather is still unsettled as No 60009 nears Druimuachdar Summit with the return *Osprey Express* bound for Edinburgh. The location is just south of Dalwhinnie.

On leaving Newtonmore southbound trains face an almost continuous climb for around fifteen miles before the summit at Druimuachdar (1,484 feet above sea level) is reached. Northbound trains face a similar challenge on leaving Blair Atholl some sixteen miles to the south of the summit. Both sections are very steeply graded, the steepest on the northbound being 1 in 70 and southbound the maximum is 1 in 80. In steam days double heading was a common sight on the heavier passenger and goods trains.
LES NIXON

132. *Above* On 12 June 1982 No 5025 is framed by a bridge as it climbs the final few miles of the 1 in 80 gradient up to Druimuachdar summit with an Aviemore–Perth special.
D. J. O'ROURKE

133. *Below* A busy scene at Inverness on the morning of 4 April 1986 as Class 47/4 No 47550 *University of Dundee* arrives with the 0740 from Aberdeen. Also in the scene is Class 47/4 No 47430 which is waiting to take out the *Clansman* – the 1030 Inverness–Birmingham New Street.

The next three scenes were taken on 12 June 1982 when No 5025 worked from Perth–Aviemore and return with the *Speyside Express*.

134. *Top left* No 5025 and the northbound special thread the famous pass of Killiekrankie. DAVID WILCOCK

135. *Bottom left* The return special is seen heading south once again in the beautiful pass of Killiekrankie. DAVID WILCOCK

136. *Top right* After working in from Perth the Black 5 is turned on the former Kyle of Lochalsh turntable at the Strathspey Railway's Aviemore depot. DAVID WILCOCK

Next pages

137. *Top left* On 4 April 1986 Class 47/4 No 47470 crosses a viaduct near Tomatin with the 1335 Glasgow Queen Street–Inverness. A journey of 180 miles which will be completed in just under four hours.

138. *Bottom left* The viaduct at Slochd provides a complete contrast to the previous picture being of stone and brick construction with elliptical arches.

The snow is still on the hills as Class 47/4 No 47438 crosses the viaduct on 4 April 1986 with the 1230 Inverness–Perth–Glasgow Queen Street. Slochd summit which is just off the top right hand edge of the picture (to the right of the power lines) is the summit of the climb from Inverness in the north and Aviemore to the south. Both climbs have gradients as steep as 1 in 60 necessitating much double heading in steam days.

139. *Top right* Class 47/0 No 47205 crosses the southern portals of the mighty Culloden Moor viaduct with the 0706 Edinburgh–Inverness service. 4 April 1986.

This 29 arch viaduct was one of the most expensive engineering features on the Highland Railway.

140. *Bottom right* No 5025 with the six coach *Speyside Express* nears Druimuachdar summit on its journey from Perth to Aviemore. 20 July 1981. JOHN COOPER-SMITH

141. *Above* On 3 October 1983 No 5025 leaves Aviemore with the 1600 for Boat of Garten on the Strathspey Railway. This former Highland Railway line ran from Aviemore to Forres on the HR Inverness–Elgin–Keith route which now forms part of the Inverness–Aberdeen main line.

142. *Right* The 1400 to Aviemore leaves Strathspey Railway's terminus at Boat of Garten with No 5025 in charge. 3 October 1983.

143. *Top left* Class 47/4 No 47620 leaves the picturesque river bridge at Blair Atholl on 12 April 1985 and approaches the station with the 0925 Edinburgh–Inverness. TOM HEAVYSIDE

144. *Bottom left* Sunday at Blair Atholl. Class 25 No 25059 in the station yard. 3 October 1983.

145. *Above* Winter on the Highland line nearly always means snow as can be seen in this picture taken from the train on 7 February 1986. The train is the 1430 Inverness–Edinburgh hauled by Class 37 No 37114 and the locomotive is near Druimuachdar summit. DAVID NIXON

146. *Below* Class 47/4 No 47430 pulls into Aviemore station with the 1630 Inverness–Perth–Edinburgh on 3 April 1986. The down platform is now very rarely used, north and southbound trains now all using the up platform.

147. *Above* Inverness still boasts very fine semaphore signals as can be seen in this picture of No 5025 and support coach approaching the station on 4 October 1982. The locomotive had come down from Aviemore in order to work a series of special trains to Kyle of Lochalsh (see next section).

148 and 149. *Right Evening Star* and *Green Arrow* pose on the turntable at the northern end of Perth station after working in with ECS of a special from Edinburgh to Gleneagles. 7 April 1986.

The Highland Main Line to Inverness is on the left hand side of both the pictures. K. J. C. JACKSON

Next page

150. *Top* Stanley Junction, seven miles to the north of Perth, on 16 June 1966 is the setting as A2 Pacific No 60532 *Blue Peter* glides through with the 1.30 p.m. Aberdeen–Glasgow train – the *Grampian* and joins the Highland Main Line which comes in from the left.

The old Caledonian route from Perth to Aberdeen is now closed between Stanley Junction and Kinnaber Junction, trains now using the coast route via Dundee and Montrose.

151. *Bottom* On 20 June 1966 Class 5MT No 44997 (shedded at Perth 63A) accelerates smartly away from Perth station with the 9.50 a.m. stopping train to Aberdeen.

This departure followed quickly behind the 8.25 a.m. Glasgow–Aberdeen three hour express which was usually hauled by one of the remaining A4 Pacifics.

For the first seven miles of its journey it will share tracks with the Highland Main Line which branches off at Stanley junction (see above).

SECTION SIX

INVERNESS TO KYLE OF LOCHALSH

This former Highland Railway line runs over eighty miles through some of the wildest and most beautiful parts of the country. It is single all the way with occasional passing loops. In steam days, locomotives used to have the automatic tablet-exchange apparatus fixed by the cab doors.

Inverness station, opened in 1856, is built of pale gold sandstone. A freshly-painted town's coat-of-arms looks very smart on the concourse. Behind the station to the south west rises the castle, built in 1834, of red sandstone – not the original which was blown up in the Jacobite rebellion. The spire of St Andrew's Cathedral can be seen behind, also of recent construction since the earthquake of 1816.

Our line bends sharp left as we leave the platforms, passing the site of the former HR works, then Rose Street signal box and junction. An industrial spur runs to the right as we rise over the river on Ness viaduct, also built of golden sandstone with nine elegant flat arches. To the north we can see down the harbour reach known as "The Cherry" to a great new road bridge over the Beauly Firth, which by-passes Inverness. This runs over the site of the former municipal airport. To the south we can see Waterloo Bridge, and on the other side of the river lies "Clachnacuddin" football ground.

On the left, a branch used to run round to Muirtown Basin on the Caledonian Canal. This picturesque "white elephant" was begun by Telford in 1805, opened (and closed) in 1822 and reopened in 1847, by which time the railways were in supremacy and shipping had developed too great a tonnage to use it. It still carries pleasure craft, etc.

We cross the canal by a hand-operated swing bridge at Clachnaharry, near the outer sea locks, and continue west through the closed stations of Bunchrew, Lentran (where there is a loop) and Clunes; from Clachnaharry to the last, the line used to be a double track. On crossing the River Beauly by a girder bridge, we turn north through Beauly station, now closed. (From Mary Queen of Scots' comment "Quel beau lieu").

The line continues north across the neck of the Black Isle, passing a grain terminal spur to the east and reaches Muir of Ord station. A loop is all that remains of the branch to Fortrose. A distillery lies on the west side, and further inland is Brahan castle, once home of the famous seer.

We cross the Conon bridge on five skew spans of masonry and run through its former station at the head of Cromarty Firth. Further on we pass the site of a shed on the left, and arrive at Dingwall, the county town of Ross-shire. The tower on the hill to the south west commemorates General Sir Hector McDonald's African campaigns. The charming station is built of light yellow stone, and the canopy has unusual fans in the glazing.

Close by the waters of the Firth the line divides, the northern route going to Wick and Thurso while our line turns west, overlooked by Tulloch castle to the north. Here we start climbing into the mountains. After a few miles, at Fodderty junction there used to be a two and a half mile branch on the left to Strathpeffer, a Victorian spa. We ascend more steeply to the former station of Achterneed. Just south of here stands Castle Leod, now conspicuous by its great parkland trees. A climb of 1 in 50 brings us through thick plantations to Raven's Rock summit at 458 ft.

The pass descends as steeply on the other side. To the south are the picturesque Rogie Falls near the road to Contin. We drop rapidly to Loch Garve and skirt its southern shore to Garve station with its passing loop set in sheltering trees. The A832 bridge crosses over the west end, by the war memorial cross. Much of the road westwards is now single, with passing places. The great bulk of mountain to the north is Ben Wyvis, 3,429 ft high.

We climb again at 1 in 50 to Corriemuillie summit at 429 ft and descend to the north shores of Loch Luidart. The station of that name is set in Strath Bran, a wild and desolate place of bog and moorland, where we may hope to see red deer and golden eagles.

After a short climb of 1 in 50, our line snakes to the south of Loch a'Chuilinn and north of Loch Achanalt, where the station is open. The great peak of Sgurr a'Mhuilinn rises 2,778 ft in the south. We climb up the valley floor to Achnasheen station, which the staff make very attractive with flowering currants, etc. There is a passing loop here by the River Bran. Ahead lies Loch a'Chroisg, shadowed by Fionn Bheinn, 3,059 ft, and Meall a'Chaoruinn, 2,313 ft, to the north.

Another stiff climb up 1 in 55 brings us to Luib summit, at 646 ft the top of the pass. A similar drop south westwards takes us down the side of Glen Carron overlooking the south shore of Loch Sgarmhain, while the road takes the north shore. The wooded banks make a pretty frame for two islands. The slopes of Coille Bhan, part of Carn Breac, 2,223 ft, hem in the glen on the

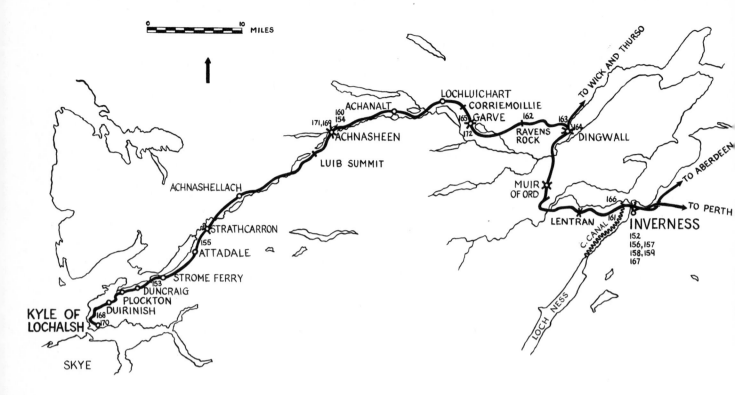

north side behind the former platform at Glen Carron Lodge, where we cross the river. We follow down the narrow pass at 1 in 50. On the left a stream, Allt a'Chronais, joins us in the woods. Its narrow gorge gives us a spectacular view of Sgurr a'Chaorachain, 3,445 ft high. We continue our steep descent to Achnashellach station, by Loch Dughaill, lying between Fuar Tholl, 2,975 ft, to the north, and Carn Mor, 1,305 ft, to the south.

As we gain the open valley floor we run through a level crossing by Balnacra school. A mile brings us to the bridge over the River Carron, and another mile to Strathcarron station, the last loop before Kyle. This cluster of buildings at the head of the estuary is sometimes called "Jeantown". The A890 takes the north shore to Strome castle, while the line hugs the slopes of the southern shore. Round the first shoulder we pass Attadale House, with its cave and pier, opposite Slumbay harbour. As we cross the River Attadale, we look up through the glacier moraine to the peaks of Ben Killilan, 2,466 ft. Behind these lie the famous "Five Sisters of Kintail".

Four miles along the water's edge brings us to Stromeferry station, where the A890 crosses the line by an overbridge by the hotel, and zig-zags south to meet the A87. The ferry connects to Strome Castle and the youth hostel opposite, under the sharp fin of Bad a'Chreamha, 1,296 ft. As we round the next headland, the loch is littered with tiny islands, some with navigation lights. Another mile takes us past Duncraig Castle and its station and slipway. Shortly afterwards, we run through Plockton station serving the harbour on the right. We cut across the end of another little bay and reach Duirnish station. This is set in National Trust land, like most of this end of the peninsula and the tiny islands. It is a marvellous place for bird-watching.

The line twists in and out of the coves for three miles and finally comes to the end at Kyle of Lochalsh. This station was opened in 1897. The terminus serves the ferry to Skye just across the sound, landing at Kyleakin. McBrayne's used to sail to Tarbert on Harris & Lewis directly, but now they sail only from Vig on the far end of Skye. There used to be many trains to meet these sailings and collect landings of fish. A few sidings still remain. The mountains behind Kyleakin are called the Cuillins, and the nearest tall peak is Beinn na Caillich. Their spectacular skylines make a fitting end for this remarkable journey.

152. *Right* Class 5MT 4-6-0 No 5025 receives admiring glances as it waits to leave Inverness with the Toyota train to Kyle of Lochalsh. 5 October 1982.

A series of private charters from Inverness to Kyle were run on four consecutive days from 4 to 7 October for the Toyota Car Company who had been promoting new designs on the Isle of Skye.

153. *Top left* On May 29 1982 No 5025 ran a special seven coach train from Inverness to Kyle of Lochalsh – the first steam train on this beautiful line for over twenty years.

The special train which was chartered by the Scottish Chamber Orchestra, is seen on the outward trip skirting Loch Carron to the west of Stromeferry. DAVID WILCOCK

154. *Bottom left* No 5025 is seen with the Inverness–Kyle of Lochalsh special on 5 October 1982 crossing the River Bran between Achanalt and Achnasheen.

155. *Above* The Toyota special for Kyle of Lochalsh hauled by No 5025 has just left Strathcarron and is beginning what is perhaps the most scenic section of the line, the twelve miles or so that skirt Loch Carron. 5 October 1982.

156. *Top left* No 5025 shunts the empty coaching stock for the special excursion to Kyle of Lochalsh. 5 October 1982.

On the right is Class 37 No 37025 with a mid-morning train to Wick and Thurso. For the first nineteen miles Kyle and Wick trains share the same track, the junction of the lines being just north of Dingwall.

Inverness station is at the apex of a triangle, Perth and Aberdeen platforms facing east and Kyle platforms north.

157. *Bottom left* Contrast in front ends at Inverness. 5 October 1982.

158. *Above* The Inverness area still has many fine semaphore signals and boxes. No 5025 and support coach poses by Inverness Rose Street box on 4 October 1982 before taking out the first Toyota special to Kyle of Lochalsh.

The lines in the left foreground form the base of the station triangle as well as being a through route from the Perth and Aberdeen lines to Kyle and the far north lines.

159. *Below* Class 37 No 37416, complete with Highland logo approaches Inverness on the morning of 4 April 1986 with the 0710 from Kyle of Lochalsh, a journey of 82¼ miles.

160. *Top left* The Strathspey Railway's Black 5 together with the Toyota special of 5 October 1982 travels through the rugged but beautiful countryside east of Achnasheen and heads for Kyle of Lochalsh.

The river in the background is the Bran which the line follows until Achnasheen.

161. *Bottom left* A birds eye view of the Scottish Chamber Orchestra special of 29 May 1982 as it leaves behind the Highland capital of Inverness. The train is approaching the swing bridge over the mouth of the Caledonian Canal at Clachnaharry. In the background is Beauly Firth which runs into the Murray Firth. The road bridge over Beauly Firth has now been completed giving travellers from Inverness to and from the north of Scotland considerable savings in time and mileage. DAVID WILCOCK

162. *Above* Shortly after leaving the junction at Dingwall, Kyle trains are faced with a very stiff climb up to Ravens Rock summit, nearly four miles at 1 in 50. On 5 October 1982 No 5025 and the Toyota special to Kyle blast their way up to Raven's Rock summit. JOHN COOPER-SMITH

163. *Above* Dingwall still boasts a very fine station complete with platform canopies, a Highland Railway style footbridge and at the time this picture was taken (5 October 1982) a very fine signal box and semaphore signals, and to complete the scene No 5025 hurries through the station with a special train bound for the Kyle of Lochalsh.

164. *Below* English Electric Class 37 No 37183 in charge of the 1110 Kyle–Inverness train is given the 'right away' at Dingwall on a sunny 20 August 1983. The Class 37s are now in charge of nearly all the Kyle and Wick trains with the exception of the odd working by Class 26s.

165. *Top right* No 5025 and the special excursion to Kyle of Lochalsh pull out of Garve station on 4 October 1982.

Garve, some twelve miles out of Dingwall, is situated at the foot of a two and a half mile climb up to Corriemuillie summit which is mainly at 1 in 50/60. Note the signal box and footbridge.

Dingwall to Kyle is single line throughout so obviously crossing places like the one at Garve are very essential.

166. *Bottom right* Black 5 and the Kyle special of 29 May 1982 pull through Clachnaharry with the outward train. Once again dominating the background is the road bridge over the Beauly Firth.
DAVID EATWELL

Previous page

167. *Top left* The bridge over the River Ness at Inverness is the location as the Toyota special of 5 October 1982 crosses it and heads for Dingwall and the Kyle of Lochalsh.

168. *Bottom left* No 5025 runs back light engine to Inverness on 5 October 1982. The locomotive has just left Kyle of Lochalsh and the Isle of Skye provides a splendid backdrop. JOHN COOPER-SMITH

169. *Right* On the Kyle trips the locomotive took water from the River Bran at Achnasheen, this location is roughly halfway between Inverness and the Kyle.
    The clouds gather as No 5025 takes water at this spot on 4 October 1982.

This page

170. Journey's end for No 5025 and the Toyota train as they enter the delightful Highland Railway terminus at Kyle of Lochalsh on 5 October 1982. The hills of Skye complete a splendid setting.

Next page

171. *Top* Class 37 No 37262 pauses at Achnasheen on Sunday, 21 August 1983 with the 0930 Inverness–Kyle of Lochalsh service. On Sundays this is the only down train of the day, the up service being the 1400 from Kyle of Lochalsh. It is only in recent years that there has been a Sunday service on this line.

172. *Bottom* Garve station 25 September 1982. Class 5MT No 5025 has just arrived with a special from Inverness and is about to be crossed by the morning Kyle–Inverness train hauled by a Class 26 locomotive complete with snow ploughs.
K. J. C. JACKSON

SECTION SEVEN

FORT WILLIAM TO MALLAIG

FORT WILLIAM TO MALLAIG

Fort William was named after William of Orange and established in 1690 on an earlier fort built by General Monk during the Commonwealth as a strategic base in the Highlands, situated on a sea loch some sixty miles inland from the ocean. The first station opened in 1894 and the original line, the Caledonian from Glasgow Queens Street via Crianlarig, passed through the gateway of the fort. This soon had to be demolished to make room for the engine sheds, but was rebuilt as the gateway to the cemetery. The present station, opened in 1975, is further north by the mouth of the Water of Nevis. The first station used to connect with McBrayne's steamers at the piers in the centre of the town. At one time there were plans to run an ocean going service to Quebec from Fort William. Now the site of the sidings is used as a bypass for the congested High Street and runs between the water and the shops.

To the south east, Ben Nevis at 4,406 feet completely dominates the town. A scheme to run a rack railway up a 1 in 2.62 gradient up the pony trail to the observatory on the summit, and build a hotel there, came to nothing. Two vast pipelines bend down the nearest side from Loch Treig in the Nevis horseshoe; these are part of a hydro-electric scheme and supply the British Aluminium Company works on the north side of Fort William. BAC then send their output to Burntisland in Fife.

The Mallaig line began as a short spur, one and three-quarter miles long on a gradient of 1 in 24, to the pier at the top of Banavie locks to speed the transit of passengers from the Caledonian canal. The West Highland Railway (Mallaig extension) reached the west coast at the turn of this century. It later became the North British and then the LNER. Some steam specials use a rake of Mark 1 coaches painted in LNER green and cream.

On departing from the station we pass under the bridge of a disused mineral line from Glen Spean, then meet the line from Glasgow at what was formerly Banavie junction and is now Mallaig junction. The sheds lie to the left and the spur to BAC comes off the Glasgow line very near on the right. We make a broad turn from northwards to westwards and pass the ruins of the castle and battlefield of 1645 on the right. We cross the River Lochy on a viaduct built of flat girders laid on crenellated stone piers which match the castle nearby.

We run over the mouth of the Caledonian canal on a swing bridge at the foot of a flight of eight locks rising 64 feet, known as "Neptune's Staircase", where the two lochs Linnhe and Eil meet in a sharp bend. Immediately afterwards we pass through Banavie station, and through an industrial area on the flat land at the head of the loch. There is a spur on the left to the Wiggins Teape paper mills, closed in 1980 with plans to reopen. This carried china clay from Cornwall and logs for pulping.

Turning due west to follow the north shore of Loch Eil, we pass through Corpach station, overlooked by the 2,420 feet peak of Stob a'Ghrianain. Apart from a 1 in 100 near Glen Suileag inlet, we run fairly level to reach Locheilside station. At the 13 mile post we leave Loch Eil, cross the stream Fionn Dubh and ascend the pass Coille Druim na Saille up 1 in 60. At the top we cross over the River Dubh Lighe and the A830. In the hillside to the right is Loch Dubh which was dammed to supply power to a turbine drill during the construction of the line. There were some hundred cuttings to excavate.

We keep close to the River Callon and pass through a short tunnel – there are eleven on this route – and come onto Glenfinnan viaduct over the River Finna at the head of Loch Shiel. This spectacular structure is built of concrete, which was 30% cheaper than the intractable local granite. The contractor, Robert McAlpine, was henceforth known as "Concrete Bob". It has 21 spans of a standard 50 feet length and carries the track 100 feet off the ground. It is 1,248 feet long and curves on 12 chain radius, requiring a 25 mph restriction. The speed limit to Mallaig is 30 mph and back to Fort William, 40 mph. Story has it that inside one of the hollow piers there are the remains of a horse and cart which slipped off the gangway during construction. There is a monument below on the shore like a lighthouse to mark Bonnie Prince Charlie's landing in 1745 to challenge the English.

Just after the viaduct is Glenfinnan station and a passing loop by the hotel . We run underneath the road bridge and ascend the narrow wooded pass following the River Abhainn Shatach to the summit at 18½ miles. The view to the south is blocked by the great bulk of Ben Odhar Mhor at 2,854 feet. We drop down 1 in 48 following the stream Allt Lon a'Mhuidhe, to a more level section where we hug the south shore of Loch Eilt with its pretty wooded islands. At the west end we pass under the road bridge, and follow the River Ailort down to Lochailort station. There is a monument on the right half-way down the pass and then a view of the peak of Moidart to the south.

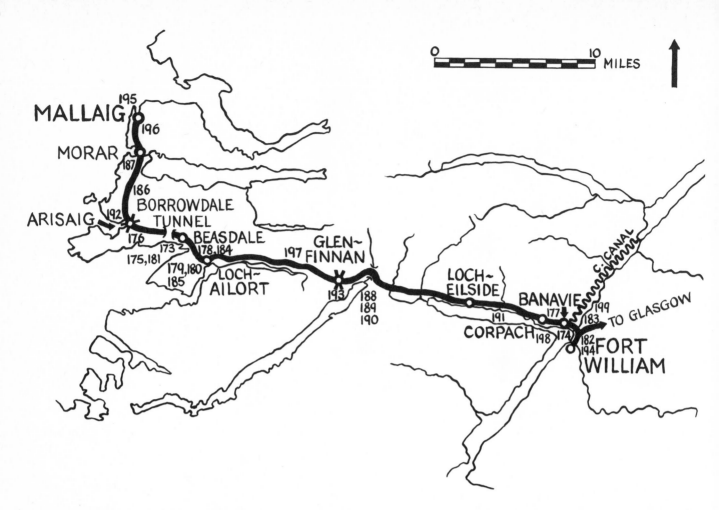

Loch Ailort shows a dramatic change of climate. A journey in spring may find Fort William surrounded by snowy peaks while the west coast, thanks to the Gulf Stream, is ablaze with flowers. Even orange seaweed on the shore lends a tropical air to the intense green of the meadows.

The next 8½ miles contain some wonders of engineering in the construction of nine tunnels and many concrete viaducts. A gradient of 1 in 50 takes us through three tunnels to the south side of Loch Dubh in the neck of Ardnish peninsula, at 26½ miles.

At Polnish a conspicuous white-washed chapel overlooks the loch near Arnabol viaduct, then the line crosses over the road and Gleann Mama river. After several tunnels we come out over the road and Beasdale Water ascending 1 in 48 to Beasdale station, the set-down point for Arisaig House. The next viaduct of eight arches, at the head of Loch Nan Uamh, crosses over the road and the line plunges into Borrowdale tunnel, the longest in this section. At the other end is the remarkable Borrowdale Bridge over Borrowdale Burn behind Arisaig house. This is 86 feet high with a rise of 22 feet. It has two side spans of 20 feet each and a great central span of 127½ feet. This was the subject of much interest in engineering journals of the day.

After the summit at 81½ miles we drop 1 in 50 to Arisaig station with a passing loop by the harbour. The climate is mild enough for palm trees here. To the north of Arisaig the line swings round through Keppoch Moss and the stream Allt cam Carach. This was crossed by means of a viaduct like the one on Rannoch Moor, but sunken, which used 70½ feet steel spans on firmly-bedded piers instead of a causeway.

At Morar station the line crosses the Falls of Morar by a bridge with a main span of 90 feet. The road crosses between this bridge and the ruined piers of an earlier road bridge in the rapids. To the seaward side a long inlet reveals the silver sands for which Morar is famous, while beyond the Sound of Sleat rise the islands Rhum, Muck and Eigg.

We reach Mallaig station after 41 miles, passing a coastguard lookout station as we approach the platforms. The station abuts the quayside for the ferry to these islands and to Kyle of Lochalsh. It was opened in 1901 and besides passenger traffic it was much used for taking fish to Billingsgate and sheep and cattle to Glasgow etc. Now the only freight seems to be a once-weekly oil tanker train to fuel the trawlers and lifeboat.

173. *Above* What better way to start the last and perhaps the most scenic section of this book than with a fine portrait of Class 5MT No 44767 *George Stephenson* in charge of a Fort William–Mallaig train at the summit of Beasdale bank. This bank although short in length (just two miles) has a ruling grade of 1 in 48 and is situated twelve miles from Mallaig. 1 July 1985. JOHN COOPER-SMITH

174. *Above* No 44767 crosses the River Lochy at Fort William at the start of the 41½ mile journey to Mallaig. 30 June 1985.

The southern slopes of Ben Nevis, the highest mountain in the British Isles at 4,406 feet, are on the left hand side of the picture. JOHN COOPER-SMITH

175. *Right* Someone once described this scene very appropriately as a Wagnerian setting. This most splendid of locations is the viaduct at the head of Loch-Nan-Uamh near Glen Beasdale.

Ian Storey's Black 5 No 44767 complete with outside Stephenson link motion and Timken roller bearings is in charge of the Mallaig–Fort William train on 27 August 1984. LES NIXON

176. *Top left* Semaphore signals complete with North British Railway posts frame Class 37 No 37112 as it enters Arisaig on 22 August 1983 with the 1630 Fort William–Mallaig train.

177. *Bottom left* Class 37 No 37408 approaches Banavie on 5 April 1986 with the 1405 Fort William–Mallaig train.

178. *Above* It is 0630 on the morning of 31 May 1985 as Class 37 No 37188 with the annual weedkilling train is photographed near Lochailort on its way to Mallaig for spraying on the return leg.
LES NIXON

179. *Top left* Reflections at Loch Eilt on 5 April 1986 as No 44767 heads for Fort William with a return special excursion from Mallaig.

180. *Bottom left* When steam returned to the West Highland line at the end of May 1984 appropriately for this former North British line, North British 0-6-0 No 673 *Maude* (together with Black 5 No 5407) was called upon to haul the first trains. Here we see *Maude* at Loch Eilt on 28 May returning to Fort William. Sadly the veteran locomotive (almost a hundred years old) failed to reach Mallaig; getting only as far as Arisaig. DAVID EATWELL

181. *Above* There is still snow on the hills as No 44767 crosses the viaduct at the head of Loch-Nan-Uamh with a return special from Mallaig. 5 April 1986.
This location is between Beasdale and Lochailort.

Next page
182. *Top left* A view of the depot at Fort William on 19 July 1985 with the two Class 5MTs Nos 5407 and 44767 dominating the scene. JOHN COOPER-SMITH

183. *Bottom left* A fine action portrait of No 44767 as it blasts away from Fort William with the 1110 to Mallaig on 21 July 1984. BRIAN DOBBS

184. *Right* 0-6-0 No 673 *Maude* throws out a fine exhaust as it climbs Beasdale bank with a train from Fort William on 28 May 1984. JOHN LAVERICK

185. *Top left* No 44767 skirts Loch Eilt on 1 July 1985 with a Fort William–Mallaig train. JOHN COOPER-SMITH

186. *Bottom left* On 22 July 1985 No 44767 descends Keppoch bank at Kinlord near Mallaig. The islands of Rhum (right) and Eigg (left) are in the distant background.

   Note the coaching stock, this rake having been specially painted LNER green and cream tourist colours. JOHN COOPER-SMITH

187. *Above* No 44767 crosses the viaduct at Morar (famous for its white sands) with the 1800 Mallaig–Fort William on Sunday, 21 July 1985. JOHN COOPER-SMITH

Next pages
188. Class J36 0-6-0 No 673 *Maude* nears the summit of the 1 in 50 climb up to Glenfinnan station on 28 May 1984. On the bottom right hand side of the picture can be seen the edge of Glenfinnan viaduct. LES NIXON

189. *Left* On 2 June 1985 No 44767 with a SLOA Fort William-Mallaig train is seen leaving Glenfinnan viaduct on the steep climb up to Glenfinnan station. JOHN COOPER-SMITH

190. *Above* A broadside view of Glenfinnan viaduct on 22 July 1985 as No 44767 heads for Fort William with a train from Mallaig. JOHN COOPER-SMITH

Next pages

191. *Top left* No 44767 and the rake of green and cream coaches, forming the 1110 Fort William–Mallaig service, skirt the shores of Loch Eilt near Fassfern. 26 May 1985. LES NIXON

192. *Bottom left* Pictured on May 28 1984, is the first steam hauled public train arriving at Arisaig en route from Fort William to Mallaig. The locomotive is Paddy Smith's Black 5 No 5407.
TOM NOBLE

193. *Top right Maude* at Glenfinnan station on 20 July 1984 waiting to return to Fort William. TOM HEAVYSIDE

194. *Bottom right* No 44767 shunts empty stock at Fort William station on 21 July 1984.
   This is a comparatively new station, the previous station being situated some distance to the southwest of this location near the riverside piers. BRIAN DOBBS

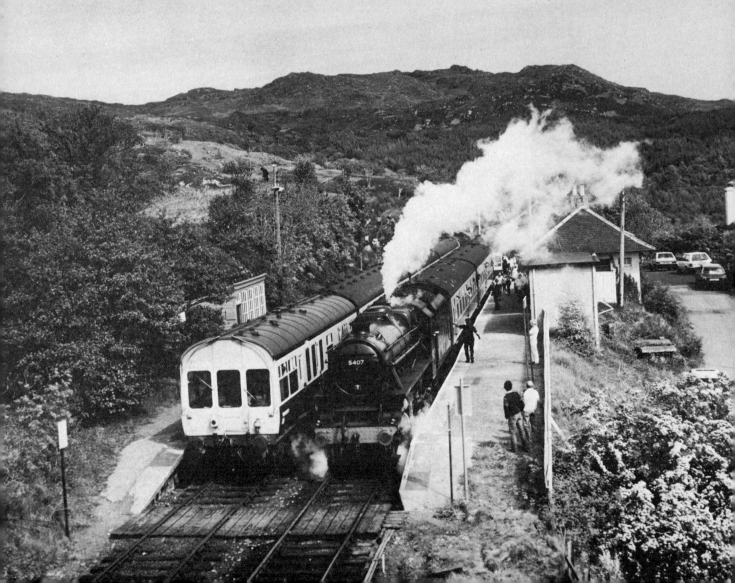

195. *Top left* The train from Fort William has just arrived at Mallaig station and No 44767 receives admiring glances from passengers and sightseers alike. 19 July 1984. TOM HEAVYSIDE

196. *Bottom left* Mallaig station on the afternoon of 22 August 1983 with Class 37 No 37188 waiting to leave on the 1615 service to Fort William. Note the former LNER observation coach at the rear of the train.

197. *Above* Class 37 No 37039 approaches Glenfinnan with the 1855 Mallaig–Fort William train. 18 June 1982. TOM HEAVYSIDE

198. *Below* A snow covered Ben Nevis overlooks No 44767 as it approaches Banavie with a special excursion to Mallaig. 5 April 1986.

199. Fort William shed, 5 April 1986.